GH00982852

ULT - OMA DRAWNINGS

NOVEMBER

UNIVERSAL Materials

SEATTLE

UNIVERSAL Materials SEATTLE

Materials SPL

TENERIFE Archive

UNIVERSAL | Consultant Drawings | ET

UNIVERSAL | File Copies | AUS

UNIVERSAL | OMA / HRA File

UNIVERSAL | Curtain Walls

UNIVERSAL | Misc. Mark-up Sets

THIS IS A PORTO
SAMPLE

PLEASE KEEP INTACT

Made by the Office for Metropolitan Architecture:
An Ethnography of Design

010 Publishers Rotterdam 2009

Made by the Office for Metropolitan Architecture:

An Ethnography of Design

Albena Yaneva

For Bruno Latour

I would like to thank my publisher for encouraging me to systematically explore the large pile of interviews and ethnographic materials collected during my participant observation in the Office for Metropolitan Architecture in Rotterdam (OMA) in the period 2002-4.

I thank the architects from the OMA for their readiness and enthusiasm to participate in such a non-conventional enquiry and for passionately sharing with me both their views on architecture and their mundane preoccupations.

A grant from the Graham Foundation for Advanced Studies in the Fine Arts in Chicago and a scholarship from the Max Planck Institute for the History of Science in Berlin enabled the fieldwork in Rotterdam. The Manchester Architecture Research Centre at the University of Manchester provided a stimulating environment for completing the research and writing.

Table of Contents

After scribbling hectically in my notebook, I stare at the big poster of the Astor building[1] hanging on a wall in Rem's office in Rotterdam; my hand pauses for a while, my eyes carefully inspect all the objects around me. Then I hide behind the notes again. We discuss the non-modernist approach to the façade of the building, other ongoing projects and approaches to design;[2] my hand again scribbles excited notes on the page; my eyes stray around the office to identify other images of OMA[3] buildings and traces of design. Whenever my hand stops, my eyes start strolling again, inspecting the office. It is an ordinary office, but it has two doors and two glass walls. One door, to the left of Rem, connects him with the secretaries' office; another larger glass door and a glass wall are facing him, separating yet simultaneously visually connecting up with the studio open-plan and the small-scale scenery of the designing architects at the OMA. The second glass wall behind Rem opens his office to the vast urban scenery of Rotterdam. Like two transparent membranes, these walls separate him from and help him immerse in two different rhythms – the slow Dutch cadence of urban life out there seen through the glass wall behind Rem, and the busy office rhythm seen through the glass wall facing him. Whenever he looks at the splendid scenery outside, Holland is out there for him – all the places where he lived, all the people for whom he designed and built. Whenever he stares at the office inside, the entire world is in here – Seattle, Cordoba, New York, Porto, Beijing, Saint Petersburg – placed on different tables of models,[4] sharing the same flat office space regardless

1 Astor Place Hotel, New York, USA, 1999; Boutique Ian Schrager hotel in Manhattan in collaboration with Herzog and de Meuron; commission.

2 On Koolhaas's non-modernist approach, see Latour, 2005a.

3 Rem Koolhaas, Madelon Vriesendorp, Elia and Zoe Zenghelis founded the Office for Metropolitan Architecture (OMA) in 1975. They signed their projects and images under the mysterious acronym OMA. The OMA in Rotterdam was opened in 1980.

of any geographic distances – waiting to be reinvented by design.

Once in the office, a tiny question lingered in my mind for a while: 'Where is his drawing pad?' In his office, there were many books, large panels of different OMA buildings, material samples and models, but there was no drawing board. The tiny question then grew into a bigger one: 'Does Rem Koolhaas draw at all?' The question holds a provocation, though provocation is precisely what Rem taught me to value the most for two years of participant observation in his office. If I am to argue that he does not draw just because I have never seen him drawing, what does this tell us about the nature of design in the OMA or the specificity of their buildings? Whenever it looks like Rem is drawing he is usually scribbling on a printed diagram or making a plan to correct it, or selecting one design option among many, or giving input to the design process to further direct design reflection. Why have I never seen him drawing but just scribbling like an anthropologist would do? Is it because most of present-day architects do not draw? Or, at least Pritzker prize laureates? This is not entirely true. Frank Gehry draws, Zaha Hadid draws, and we can extend this list. In their offices, design is launched by a conceptual sketch made by the master architect and this is furthered by many other drawing hands and with the help of AutoCAD and other software. The younger designers will spend days and nights trying to achieve the same shade of grey or black as Zaha Hadid,[5] or the same curved outlines as the ones produced by the creative thinking that 'let Frank Gehry's designer's hand trace the mind's non-preconceived intentions that go beyond the limits of the human imagination'.[6] Triggered by a single slight of hand, in a moment of quasi-artistic inspiration but reproduced, repeated, retouched and corrected many times, slightly altered, versioned, rendered, rescaled, and displaced, the building emerges as a collective product, yet often signed by the same hand that drew the first sketches. These are, 'Rembrandt-like' workshops[7] where the building arises as a cumulative result of repetitions, corrections and adjustments of that initial set of conceptual drawings produced by the hand of a skilful master architect.

If Rem Koolhaas does not draw, or only rarely and occasionally draws, this is because design at the OMA often begins with collective experimentation at the table of models and not with a single-authored sketch; it is made by and 'is a response to a certain network'[8] of architects, engineers, contractors and consultants, drawing software and drawing hands, boards and tracing papers. Design action is distributed differently in the OMA in comparison to the practices of Hadid or Gehry. Thus, it is quite expected that an architect would not be on his own in the creative process; there is a variety of other actors, both human and non-human,[9] who participate in design and make it a heterogeneous and genuinely co-operative venture. As Rem himself states, 'it's not me, it's *made by OMA*'. A building or an urban concept that holds the stamp of OMA emerges as a relational effect of a whole network rather than as a sketch that travels and is collectively transformed, modified and translated on the way toward the final building.

Just as it is impossible to understand Rembrandt's work without understanding the aspects of his studio practice

---

4 Design at the OMA happens on different tables, which contain various scale models of a building, its parts and detailed variations. The tables are important cognitive tools and flexible organizational nodes in the process of design (Yaneva, 2009).

5 On Zaha Hadid and the importance of her design drawings and presentational strategy for the success of a project, see Crickhowell, 1997.

6 On Frank Gehry's drawing techniques, see Rappolt and Violette, 2005; Pollack, 2006; on the social use of architectural drawing, see Robbins, 1994.

7 Alpers described the Rembrandt enterprise emphasizing his specific approach of training his assistants and students to do an amazing amount of copying of drawings produced by the master in the studio; the students followed his lead in copying his drawings while he corrected and retouched the drawings, in a way that the paintings known as paradigmatic for his time were indeed painted by the hands of others rather than by Rembrandt himself as single creative genius (Alpers, 1988).

8 Interview with Ole, November 2002, OMA.

9 The term 'non-human' is used by Bruno Latour to replace 'object' as well as to widen its scope. Latour's view is that non-humans have an active role that is often forgotten or denied. He employs the terms 'human' and 'non-human' to avoid the restricted subject-object distinction and bypass it entirely (see Latour, 1999).

along with his specific handling of paint, the theatrical treatment of his models and his relationship with the market,[10] it is impossible to understand Koolhaas's work without considering his design practice. If you still find it disturbing that some of the works of a great artist, seen as paradigmatic, are painted by other hands, you will not for a moment be less confused than I was when sitting in the office with two doors, comprehending that the hands of an architect like Rem Koolhaas rarely take part in the collective process of drawing and modelling in the OMA. Realizing that, it is astounding to see architectural theorists still desperately trying to understand his style, idiosyncrasy and strengths by simply referring to his singularity and individuality as a 'creator' – to his childhood, major architectural influences upon his work, or his Dutch-ness – as if we were to judge him as an eighteenth-century unique genius. That a contemporary architect is not reducible to his autographic œuvre is nothing that would surprise designers today. Much less would the reader be amazed by a definition of architecture as a co-operative activity of architects and support personnel alike, humans and models, paints and pixels, material samples and plans, all of which constitute the *design world*.[11] Yet, such realistic accounts of contemporary architectural practices are still missing.[12]

A quick scheme or a slow story?

Shortly after I started working at the OMA,[13] I met Markus who was the head of AMO[14] at the time. He was intrigued by my study, but he could not understand why I wanted to spend so much time in the office following projects and architects at work. One day he came to me and sat on the table where I was working. He took a pencil and drew a diagram of the process. This was one of those step-by-step gradual rational design-process schemes that you often find in many books on design.

Happy with the visual result, Markus made a small 'to do' list for me to follow. He wanted to save me time by providing a quick overview of the stages of design at the

OMA: '*1* The research stage – at the end of this stage the   **13**
content is defined; *2* The concept design – the idea is
defined and the building is beautiful; *3* The schematic
design – the building is defined. The presentational books
very often exhibit the schematic design and design development; or conceptual and schematic design; *4* The design
development – the building is feasible. In design development, the building is becoming ugly and uglier, is dis-
membered into different schemes and files, and then
becomes beautiful again at the end; *5* The construction
documents – the building is executable; *6* The construction, administration and planning – the building is built;
7 Lectures, publications, exhibitions – once the building
is built.'

Thus, following what according to Markus was a well-
structured, linear and sequential process seemed to be a
very simple research task for an ethnographer.

Only after a week of participant observation did I find
out that the design process at the OMA had its own internal
rhythm and tempo, that models and plans have unpredictable trajectories, that the concept of the building is questioned whatever the stage of design may be, that there are
many rhythmic conduits through which the building devel-
ops and they would not necessarily correspond to one particular stage in the process diagram drawn by Markus. As
other architects put it: 'When you look at the process

---

10 See Alpers, 1988.

11 Here I follow Becker's understanding of the world of art as a co-operative activity
(Becker, 1974; Becker, 1982).

12 For more traditional sociological analyses of architectural firms, see Blau, 1984;
Cuff, 1991.

13 This research started as a post-doctoral project carried out in Lorraine Daston's
group at the Max Planck Institute for the History of Science in Berlin, and completed
at the Harvard University in Peter Galison's group.

14 AMO is the counterpart to OMA's architectural practice. AMO is a research studio
and think-tank that operates beyond the boundaries of architecture and urbanism
– including sociology, technology, media, and politics. It is in charge of the purely
conceptual work of architectural research, of conceptual architecture, whereas OMA
is in charge of architectural projects, or architecture built. As Ole Scheeren, partner
of OMA says, AMO is the mirror image of OMA, OMA*AMO shows the combination
of practical and theoretical intelligence.

from a distance it is a linear process, but during the design it is really hard to say where exactly we are going.'[15] Moving according to different trajectories of space and time, designers perform series of steps with various intensities and speeds. This requires taking into account the rhythms and the minute material operations of design, the materiality, the equipment and the variable ontology of the actors involved. To grapple with that mundane rhythm of design at the OMA, I needed to engage in slow observation and analysis rather than follow quickly drawn schematic diagrams of the process.[16]

Accounting for the momentum in the practice of the Office for Metropolitan Architecture (2001-4), this book offers an ethnographic glance at design. It gathers small accounts of different design trajectories, reminiscent of short stories. These are narratives I told many times while working in or presenting my work on the OMA, but which I never wrote down separately.[17] They are stories that deserve to be told. Written as such, they provide interpretations of the design process without drawing sequential linear storylines; nor do they rely on predictable narratives of events. Short stories, as a literary genre, revolve around the resolution of a conflict, a tension, a false assumption, an inversed expectation, and often have unexpected ironic or tricky endings. Similarly, concise ethnographic accounts rely on a fold in time and space to account for the distinctive features of design in this office; image patterns evoke a sense of the reality of design. The different stories follow often unconnected projects and events. Nevertheless, their sequence provides an extended story arc, progressing through accumulation. The common feature of all stories is that they all account for the nature of design invention; the latter is not reduced here to an abstract concept of creation or construction. Instead, I tackle it as something that resolves into concrete actions and practices: in collective rituals, techniques, habits and skills ingrained by training and daily repetition, in reuse of materials and recycling of historical knowledge and foam chunks. It is also a very fragile process – when a building is in the making and as long as it exists as a scale model, its existence is very tentative, very frail. At any moment in design process it can live or it can die, it can merge into something else, it can be reused, recollected. That is, a view of design as constituted from the inside; it stems from the experience of making.[18]

Why stories?

This writing strategy aims at creating a reflexive text by trying to direct attention to the reader himself, to his own life and experience as a designer. The stories are not to be read as information about how design always or often happens in the OMA (many architects' accounts today could contradict what my interviewees said in 2002 and 2003). Yet, the short stories told here will guide readers through the kind of signs and immerse them in the kind of rhythms they need to witness in order to understand what designing entails at the OMA. The good reader of such stories would not be one who asks 'Is this true? What really happened there? Is it always like this in the OMA? Would I find traces of the typical design process if I were to go to that office now and try to unravel the secrets of such a successful design practice?' Rather it would be someone who would ask the question: 'What is happening to me as the stories unfold, now, as I follow the complex trajectories of models

---

15 Discussion with Erez and Sarah, April 2002, OMA.

16 Design is commonly described in the design literature as a rational step-by-step linear process, see Jones, 1970; Heath, 1984; Rowe, 1987; Shoshkes, 1989; Lawson, 1994. The analysis in this book will circumvent the linear rational schema of design process.

17 A different study of design in the making, based on rare ethnographic materials from the OMA with a particular focus on the projects for the extension of the Whitney Museum of American Art in New York, was published in a separate book (Yaneva, 2009).

18 Some recent investigations on design practice have shown an attempt to tackle alternative thinking in architecture, but rely mainly on the designers' discourses rather than on the experiences of designing architects (see Hubbard, 1995; Mitchell, 1996; Fisher, 2000). My study is rather inspired by architectural analyses that focus on the practices of designing architects as reflective practitioners (Schön, 1983; Schön, 1985) and on the particular translations of architectural visuals on the way to the final building (Evans, 1997; Evans, 1989).

and designers at the OMA?' Design specificity is not really there, out there, any more. To recollect a moment in the office life I simply rely on the way the architects I interviewed understood design. In the process of reading, you, as a reader can also become a producer of another text that transforms, translates, embroiders and adds to the unbroken chain of interpretations of the OMA's design practice. In other words, I do not wish to offer a normal linear matter-of-fact reconstruction of the practice of OMA, recalling the different periods and generations of projects in office life,[19] recollecting the narratives of the master architect and the different cohorts of designers.[20]

The stories do not correspond to case studies from office practice, assuming that, like many social scientists would do, the findings of a case study show the larger framework within which the case is situated and by which it is ultimately determined. My stories do not aim at reaching a meta-level of explanation of design, of specific OMA buildings or of Koolhaas's style in general. In contrast, they remain self-exemplifying – they 'just' offer the world lived in the office, and depict it, deploy it, whenever the story allows. They recount how models, as virtual beings, gain a concrete reality little by little; they tell of how story-telling reveals traces of their metamorphoses, some of their *trajectories*. In my efforts to forestall certain outcomes and encourage others, I attempt to gather as many allies as possible; I challenge my 'adopted' languages and try out linguistic possibilities.

The meta-reflexive way of writing is based on the idea that the most deleterious effect of a text is to be naively believed by the reader as relating to a referent out there in some way; it is far from being productive.[21] I prefer to follow an infra-reflexive approach that goes against this common belief by asking no privilege for the account at hand. This exercise in infra-reflexive writing can be seen as a test of the short story genre in design studies. In the accounts presented here, architects and their models are free and active anthropological projects, full of life, and ready to

take part in an intriguing story; design process appears as
a reflexive and responsive event.

---

19 For such accounts see Lucan, 1991; Cuito and Montes, 2002; Patteeuw, 2004; Levene et al., 2006.

20 For interview-based reconstructions of the OMA approach, see Kwinter, 1996; Chaslin, 2001.

21 Here I follow closely Latour's distinction between meta-reflexive and infra-reflexive writing. As he put it: 'There is more reflexivity in one account that makes the world alive than in one hundred self-reference loops that return the boring thinking mind to the stage.' Latour, 1988, p. 173.

Looking at the scenery in the office, one can see the table of models of the team working on a competition entry for new NATO headquarters.[22] A couple of tables further on is the huge table with models of the China Central Television building in Beijing (CCTV),[23] and in the corner close to the shelves with materials, the Cordoba project, surrounded by Spanish speaking architects.[24] The Seattle Public Library monumental model is kept on a separate table on the ground floor,[25] while the models for the extension of the Whitney Museum of American Art in New York are displayed on another table.[26] Spread on three tables are the models of the Los Angeles County Museum of Art (LACMA),[27] whereas just one huge model of the recently completed la Casa da Musica in Porto has been kept.[28] Why were these buildings made this way? How do OMA architects come to these shapes?

A critical sociologist or anthropologist would explain the superiority of society or culture by simply introducing into the explanation higher levels of complexity, of emergent properties, of microstructures: How is American culture, for instance, embedded in the design of the Seattle Library, how are Chinese politics mirrored in the CCTV tower in Beijing, how is Portuguese culture reflected in the Casa da Musica? Are they *below* the tiny scale models or *above* them, explaining them? That is, the factors that would explain and glorify architecture by placing it on a remote pedestal do not arise within the realm of architecture. Another possible line of explanation is to elucidate Koolhaas's buildings and design approach with larger, overarching conceptual frameworks and theoretical influences: to what extent was the early Koolhaas influenced by Surrealism?[29] The impact of the Modern Movement on his design work will be recalled, his rapport with functionalism, the theoretical influence of Mies van der Rohe or le Corbusier, of Russian constructivism, of American

architecture in the 1920s and 1930s will be quoted.[30] Another storyline would follow his background as a journalist
for the *Haagse Post* and his work as a screenwriter, or his
childhood in Indonesia, connecting it with his architectural approach and trying to clarify its distinctive features.
His fascination with Manhattan and his theory of the sky-
scraper, density and congestion will be explained by his
Dutch-ness and the fact that the first settlers of Manhattan
were Dutch recreating their own country with nostalgia.[31]
And the list of interpretations can be continued; they all
revolve around these lines. The admiration of the architectural critics and theorists covers the 'symbolic' aspects
of buildings, the ideas, the subjective imagination of the
creator, whereas 'matter' is a term of depreciation, 'practice'
is seen as a synonym of banality, and 'design experience' as
trivial, as something to be explained away or apologized for.

Exploding in the world of architectural history in the
1990s, critical theory embedded itself in the discipline in
a myriad of different shapes and means. Criticizing the
studies of single architects or architectural practices as
limited and trivial,[32] it offered to use any theoretically
informed academic discipline (history, cultural studies, anthropology, geography, sociology) as a mental schema, as
'an [outer] explicit framework in which to situate the architectural objects of study'.[33] As a result, post-structuralism,

---

22 NATO, Brussels, Belgium, 2002; competition for a new, extended, fully integrated
NATO Headquarters.
23 CCTV Headquarters, Beijing, China, 2002; new headquarters and cultural centre
for China Central Television; under construction.
24 Cordoba Congress Center, Cordoba, Spain, 2002; congress centre bridging the
east and west banks of Cordoba; design stage.
25 Seattle Central Library, Seattle, USA, 2004; built.
26 Whitney Museum extension, New York, USA, 2001; concept.
27 LACMA extension, Los Angeles, USA, 2001; design proposal for extension of
the Los Angeles County Museum of Art; competition submission.
28 Casa da Musica, Porto, Portugal, 2005; concert hall for the City of Porto; built.
29 See Koolhaas, 1978; Vidler, 1992; Hill, 2003; Mical, 2005.
30 See Lucan, 1991.
31 See Damisch, 1991.
32 They rely on a limited understanding of empiricism as a blatant attempt to
trivialize architectural practice (see Colquhoun, 1981; Johnson, 1994; Hays, 1998).

feminism, psychoanalysis, (post-)Marxism, post-modern critical theory and a multitude of other formulations have changed not only the interpretative categories but also the very epistemological foundations on which architectural theory was grounded.[34] Critical theory postulated that in order to see the logical patterns of an architectural process or product, the latter should be extracted from the rather messy and irregular process of a production method full of insignificant details; one should rather go upwards until embracing higher-level theoretical frameworks outside architecture – social factors, cultures, politics. Architectural theorists pursued a wider conceptual framework for architecture, which, as many thinkers denoted, was missing: a framework that could embrace activities from patronage through to construction and use.

The main assumption of critical theory is that architecture is something capable of being inserted and understood in wider comprehensions of cultural production. Therefore, to put across the meaning and the relevance of architecture, critical studies find it necessary to position it as a historical subject within various contexts in order to be able to outline its economic, social and political dimensions, and to show that it is always directly tied to these conditions given both its scale of production and public use.[35] Be it the architecture of the Berber house of Kabyle[36] or the typical English terraced house of 1910,[37] or even the particular dwelling form of the bungalow,[38] they are all regarded as a microcosm that reflects the macrocosm of society, mimics the organization of universe, follows legal estate patterns and historical forces or dwelling habits and cultures. The small follows and reflects the big; architecture embraces the shapes suggested by society or culture. Thus, in order to be understood, buildings had to be located within the entire spectrum of economics, politics, social practices and architectural theory. The same spectra were also invited to explain the design process, the success or failure of architectural projects, and to elucidate why a particular style emerges or vanishes at a particular moment of time, or to shed light on urban dynamics and city developments. The 'broader and more inclusive' types of readings generally address 'matters of race, sexuality, class, psychoanalysis, social space, the way in which meanings are created and transferred by means of experience, political action, gender and so on'. For the critical authors, 'dealing with these kinds of things in both architectural production specifically and cultural production in general maximizes the opportunity to learn all that architecture is and might be capable of'.[39] In addition, they consider that 'to speak about architectural history without reference to these things, to other disciplines, to theory, is not only to dismiss architecture's relevance to the world in general, but also to *trivialize* [the italics are mine: AY] current conditions and preoccupations'.[40] To avoid trivialization, critical theorists engage in an exploration of architecture's hidden meanings and practices, advocating what they believe to be a 'richer and more significant' understanding of architecture. Having the ambitious task of providing a space of imaginative abstraction beyond of the immediate remits and dictates of architectural practice, the critical method consists of displacing the conventional objects of study and challenging them by referring to abstract ideas from outside architecture to explain design process, creative thinking and practices. Borrowing concepts from the critical sociology of Pierre Bourdieu, the de-constructivist approach of Jacques Derrida, or the archaeology of Michel Foucault, architectural theory assumes that its main operation consists of unveiling hidden mechanisms, constraints or representations, principles and forces behind architec-

---

33 See Borden and Rendell, 2000: 5.
34 See Leach, 1997.
35 See Tafuri, 1979; Ockman, 1985.
36 See Bourdieu, 1971.
37 See Muthesius, 1982.
38 See King, 1984.
39 See Borden and Randell, 2000: 15.
40 See Borden and Randell, 2000: 16.

tural objects, projects, and urban developments. Yet, by suggesting a theoretical outside from which conventional interpretations could be challenged, critical theory relied on the main assumption that there is a 'social context' in which architectural and urban activities take place, and which can explain their meaning and relevance.

This mirror-fashioned relationship between architecture and society[41] has as its main assumption the notion that the 'social' is a separate domain of reality that can be used as a specific type of causality to account for the 'architectural' aspects, and is supposed to give solidity, durability and consistency to the domain of architecture which it cannot maintain by itself. Although it is recognized that urban planning has its own strength and internal logic, it is assumed that some aspects of it would be better understood if some 'social dimensions' and 'social conditions' were added. Although the design process unfolds under its own logic, there are always some 'social' elements and factors to explain its unpredictable turns and difficulties. Although architectural projects develop according to their own inner drives and competitive logics, some of their more puzzling aspects and the erratic behaviour of the multitudes of actors enrolled on the way to their realization are said to pertain to several 'social influences' and 'social limitations'. Therefore, to explain a particular building or urban concept, a critical thinker would show its entrenchment in 'the social context of its time' and would present it as reminiscent of the 'political climate of an époque', of intricate power relations and economic interests. In order to elucidate the design moves and inventive impetus of architects, planners and urban developers, he or she would account for the social and political influences on these 'creators', or reflect on the instrumental role of architecture.[42]

The ambition here is different. My purpose is not to engage in another theoretical interpretation of architecture, much less to argue that social conditions or cultural perceptions are relevant to the perception and interpretation of Koolhaas's architecture. The common interpretations of OMA buildings and urban concepts isolate architecture and its appreciation by placing them in a realm of their own, disconnected from other modes of experiencing, from the stream of everyday design practice, of design living, and often arising because of extraneous conditions. The problem of these critical theory-inspired interpretations is that they start by compartmentalizing the design works in a niche apart, treating them as spiritual, as symbolic, as significant, but out of touch with the objects of design experience. These pigeon-hole theories of architecture arrest the specificity of a design work in the cultural background of the creator or the society he is designing for. They remain sterile unless they make us aware of what to seek in concrete design works, and unless they suggest the conditions under which a design work is the refining of raw materials into a valuable building-to-be. The alternative to a critical theory-inspired approach is to re-establish the connections disclosing, in pragmatic fashion, the way in which these design works come into being and the way they gain meaning in design experience. Thus, to understand the nature of architectural design at the OMA, I do not refer to the wider frameworks of Surrealism or the Modernist Movement, nor do I evoke overarching cultural and social contexts outside architecture. I rather offer a view of the architectural office from the inside in order to see and recount the multifarious aggregates that architecture links together. The OMA appears in the small ethnography

41 See King, 1980.
42 A few authors have escaped the pitfalls of a representational theory and tackled architecture as possessing the power to affect people's behaviour; they have seen its role as the one of a *pattern giver to society* (Foucault, 1979; Evans, 1982; Markus, 1993). In a number of Foucault-inspired studies, architecture and society maintain 'an instrumental relationship', and buildings are seen as mechanisms for exercising power, invisible control or punishment, expressing, giving room for, sustaining, denying or producing bonds. A growing body of recent studies on buildings pursued a stronger commitment to appraise and reconnect them with the shaping of the social, thus arguing for the conceptual weight that architecture has upon the practices in these institutions and the power of buildings to influence them (Heurtin, 1999; Galison and Thompson, 1999).

presented here as one star-like connecting site, a local place where the global, the universal values, contexts and cultures are assembled and reassembled, a place where too little can be seen, but nevertheless can be well seen.

A lot has been written about the OMA. Yet, most of the accounts cover particular projects from the first decade of its existence 1981-91 and recall the practice's metropolitan type of architecture. Different interpretations divide the life of the practice into 'American' and 'European' periods,[43] or 'surrealist' and 'scientific' phases of visualization.[44] They either attempt to synthesize the OMA's mode of thinking 'by showing all the iconographic elements indispensable to its understanding'[45] or recollect Koolhaas's own interpretations of the OMA.[46] Most of these accounts rely on interviews with the master architect, official PR material produced for the OMA (mainly project documentation composed of final images and polished interpretations) or the media stories.

Yet, no one ever attempted to spend more than a day in the practice in order to see if, by chance, he or she will bump into the ghost of Le Corbusier or feel the shadow of Mies van der Rohe on the steep staircase connecting the first and the seventh floor of the office, if he or she will randomly pop up among a bunch of surrealistic images on the office computers, if he or she will witness the distinctive approach of a glorious screenwriter in search of the generic city, or seize the quick appearances of a flying Dutchman on the way to the airport. No one ever believed that, in order to unravel what design means in this practice, more than an interview session with the star architect is needed, more than a bunch of scenarios are to be explored for a project to succeed, more than a couple of public images could be collected to reconstruct a sinuous project trajectory, more than the official media story can be told about the significance of a building. No one assumed that design, albeit in the office of a Pritzker prize winner, is *experience*. Imagination, big ideas, stylistic influences can take a rest. Society and culture can wait to be reinvented by design. As you read these lines, hundreds of architects are about to retouch the contours of an image, scale and rescale a model, stage a project presentation or visit a building site, build a mock-up, or negotiate with engineers and clients. Yes, design is a trivial, banal, mundane experience, and if we want to understand the OMA buildings this experience is to be approached with care and respect.

When we follow and recall mundane trajectories of design, does it mean that we are assuming that a model or a piece of foam are always smaller than Rotterdam, than Porto, than Seattle or any other destination of OMA projects? Does it mean their design logics can be explained by simply referring to the influences upon Koolhaas or to the societies and cultures he is designing for? Before we even begin to unravel the ontology of creativity, we should question what is big and what is small, what explains and what is to be explained. Is Portuguese society higher and more complex than a simple architectural model of the Casa da Musica in Porto? Can American culture explain the making of the Seattle Library? Is a scale model of the Whitney Museum in New York, taken in the repetitive moves of scaling up and down in the OMA, smaller than American society? Can it guide us to understanding Manhattan architecture or Rem Koolhaas's style? No, no one can claim that there is a *Zeitgeist* somewhere or a culture that could explain why the buildings of Koolhaas are made in this way.

It is not the researcher's responsibility to decide whether a scale model of the library in Seattle, or the printed panel of Hotel Astor in Rem's office are bigger than America, or whether American culture is the wider, overarching outside context that can explain why these OMA buildings are thus made. There are no pre-given explanations of design, no established scales, no recognized-by-all conceptual frames; instead, we need to devote ethnographic attention

43 See Lucan, 1991.
44 See Vidler, 1992.
45 See Lucan, 1991: p. 7.
46 See Kwinter, 1996; Chaslin, 2001, Koolhaas et al., 1995.

to what it means to design, to the many local arrangements from which creativity springs. And here I am, an ethnographer in the OMA, spending nights and days following the actors in design, carefully maintaining all my fragments of observation (interview transcripts, images, diagrams from the group discussions). I follow designers at work also because I assume that there is much more logic in each piece of work executed by them, even in the apparently insignificant and unrelated design operations such as classifying models or reusing an old and forgotten piece of foam, than in the totality of their behaviour or design philosophy.

One ought to look at design from the inside rather than observing it from a distance and gaining only a superficial view. If one follows a model or an architect in their mundane trajectories through the office, traces the small operations of recycling and reusing foam from past projects, watches how a model comes into being, is reused and circulated, one will be able to witness that they are made of a much vaster collection of entities (colour shades, humans, scaling instruments, angles of cutting, chunks of foam, pixels and paints) than the society or culture that is meant to explain them. For any so-called 'atomic' or 'small' design element to be produced, the designers have to collect and reconsider millions of pixels and colour shades. Any stabilized bunch of one-shape scale models is made of a few smaller scale models, hundreds of material samples and thousands of scaling repetitive moves. The model that might initially appear to consist of simple design elements presents itself as a much more complex entity composed of multitudes of 'little persons'; it is much bigger, always richer in difference and complexity.[47] If one follows its trajectories ethnographically, one will discover slow and gradual painstaking operations of scaling, choosing a texture, testing an old foam model, fine-tuning the colours, retouching a photo, simulating shapes. One will see humans and non-humans in a much more differentiated way, much richer in continuous mutations, transformations and vari-

ations than American culture or Dutch or Chinese societies. One will be led to believe that there is more complexity in these tiny operations than at the level of the final
building, at the level of society.

The complex monad that constitutes an architectural
office transcends the artificial being of any 'superior' order
of American, Dutch, Chinese societies or cultures, or any
other 'macro' entities. The design studio does not simply
form a microcosm, which would explain, give reason to,
or reflect the overarching macro structures. It is rather a
universe, an entire cosmos whose distinctive features I try
to unravel with ethnographic tools, whose diversity I try to
deploy in full. This implies a richer meaning of empiricism as that which is given to our experience, as William
James propagated.[48] Far from striving to envelop design
processes in as many contextual frameworks outside architecture as possible, the series of stories written in a pragmatist fashion tackle the practices of designers rather than
their theories and their ideologies.[49] They look down,
instead of going up to gain a wider panorama of theoretical
landscapes outside architecture. This is a myopic approach,
scrutinizing to the details of architectural practices.[50] Thus,
instead of taking our cue from philosophical reflection on
creativity and trying to provide, by any means, a stand-in
(social, psychological, historical or other) explanation of
design, I intend to unravel design invention here as a set
of everyday trajectories of models and architects moving
through the office space, letting themselves being transformed, leaving traces. If a *project* covers the process of
step-by-step realization of an idea, a *trajectory* accounts
for the explorations, the discoveries, the numerous detours
and unpredictable surprises that might occur. It stands for

47 As Tarde has argued 'There is more complexity at the basis of the phenomena
than at their summit.' (see Tarde, 1999, p. 39).
48 See James, 1907.
49 See Yaneva, 2005, 2009; Callon, 1996; Houdart, 2006; Houdart and Minato, 2009.
50 This approach is inspired by the understanding of architecture of Deleuze and
Guattari (see Deleuze and Guattari, 1987; Guattari, 1994); for a recent study on the
philosophy of architecture inspired by these authors, see Sloterdijk 2005.

the entire experiential dimension of the process of making of a design. It is at the same time the activation and the result of many accidental encounters. Arguing against the preconception of design as project-making and project-realization, the stories that follow will account for the *trajectorial* nature of design.[51]

To understand the meaning of OMA buildings and Koolhaas's architecture, we need to forget the architect and his building for a moment, and turn away from the official interpretations on the pages of the architectural journals or the theoretical interpretations inspired by the critical approach. We ought to ignore references to architectural theory, to society or culture as prevailing forces of explanation. We rather need to look at the ordinary forces and conditions of experience, to follow the designers in the office and the paths their work has traced. We must track the way their actions spread and the way architects make sense of their world-building activities, the routines, mistakes, and workaday choices usually considered of lesser importance for judging the meaning of a building. In so doing, we can arrive at a better understanding of OMA's design by the means of a detour to design experience. The purpose is to avoid the passage through the vague notions of society, culture, imagination, creativity, which do not explain anything but need explanation.

---

51 As design is integration of concerns of different parties, there are many other design trajectories that can be followed in an ethnography out-of-the-office. This type of approach could show how a museum model, for instance, travels and is discussed with the client, the artists, the curators, and the company that is going to run the restaurant or the shop and will incorporate all their concerns. On some of these collaborations, see Yaneva, 2009, chapter 3, pp. 151-9.

Voices

Before showing you around, before tracing the different trajectories of architects and models at the OMA, I first wish to let you hear the voices of some OMA architects reflecting upon the specificity of design in this office.[52]

'What is it that makes OMA specific, different from other architectural offices?' This was a question I asked many times and at various moments during the development of the projects I followed. I will let different architects speak: Sho, Olga, Ole, Carol, Alain and Rem; and I will introduce them briefly. Tracing the profiles of the architects I interviewed in 2002-04, while briefly sketching their career now in 2009, is like going back in time and transversally tracing the series of events and OMA projects they were engaged in, thus gaining a sense of the extent to which they were implicated in the life of the office at the time of my study. It allows me to formulate retrospectively how important their work was for the collective projects stamped 'OMA' and how these projects reciprocally shaped their individual trajectories.

Let us start with Rem's voice:

'Architecture is very flexible and almost everything is possible except flocking the building in the air. So, in a way, if you really want to do it, *you can do it in this office*.'[53]

Then we have Shohei Shigematsu. I initially met Sho when he was involved in the Whitney project, but I then had the chance to follow his work on other projects and conduct interviews with him on a variety of topics related to the OMA design approach and ongoing projects.

Shohei Shigematsu joined the Office for Metropolitan Architecture in 1998. In 2008 he became a partner of the

52 Other architects are also mentioned in the stories: Markus Dettling, Sarah Gibson, Gabriela Bojalil, Abjihit and Victoria, but they will not be introduced here as I will not refer extensively to the interviews with them to develop the stories.
53 Interview with Rem, April 2002, OMA.

OMA Holding company while still director of the OMA*AMO New York office. As such, he oversees OMA's operations in North America and is in charge of Cornell University's new building for the College of Architecture, Art and Planning in Ithaca, NY, a mixed-use high-rise building in Jersey City, NJ, and a residential tower with CAA (Creative Artist Agency) screening room on 23 East 22nd Street in Manhattan, among other projects.

He was project leader of winning design competitions such as the CCTV Headquarters in Beijing, the Koning Julianaplein mixed-use building in The Hague and the Shenzhen Stock Exchange building. He has been a driving force in conceptual projects such as the Universal Head-quarters in Los Angeles, the Whitney Museum Extension in New York, the Tokyo vertical campus, the China National Museum and Prada Epicenters for Shanghai and London.

AY: Tell me something more about the specificity of the work in the OMA. How would you compare this archi-tecture practice with other offices?

SHO: I came here after I graduated. I haven't worked in other offices. But of course you get to know how the other offices work through friends and the specificity lies in doing something like this [he points to the models around him and takes the model of the CCTV building] and taking these models seriously, trying to analyse the intention and always trying to look for new and inter-esting ideas out of very naïve-like models. I'm sure that some architects can laugh when they look at this, but we are pretty serious in analysing what is really good and what is bad, and we try to create new things. We do not think in terms of: 'OK, this is not impossible, this is possible, we are just experimenting, expressing'.

AY: Are the models the best tool for thinking and conduct-ing experiments on the building?

SHO: I don't think so. Of course in the architectural part of the OMA, it's like traditional. And also it is faster, it be-comes more suggestive, you can touch, you can really see. But I don't think that Rem excludes the possibility of using computers or whatever. It's just handier and at this moment computers are still not good enough to make really quick studies. It's also a matter of time, but if you can make really suggestive 3-D computer models, of course everybody will think it's good. You have to be strong enough to promote your method.

AY: Do you think the models in the OMA can be replaced by another tool?

SHO: They could be. For me it's already very difficult, but maybe… Yes, if you do such a study, I can't imagine doing it by a computer. Maybe some people can.

AY: And what is the role of the other tools like sketches, diagrams, and drawings in the design process in the OMA?

SHO: That's the specificity of this office – that you make a charade, you make a really big brainstorm session, and try to obtain a really clear idea from it. And this is done by using very clear diagrams so that almost everyone can immediately see what our intention is, then we can achieve something. So, often our diagrams are pretty different from those in computer-orientated offices. We use very naïve diagrams almost like cartoons in children's books. We also spend a lot of time on making books, which is also part of the presentation materials. There is also an element of clarifying things for ourselves. (…) What is may be interesting for you is that this office is quite ambitious and we always propose what we want to do. It's interesting to see how long that ambition lasts during the design process.

AY: You mean how long you are going to keep this ambition?

SHO: No, we always remain ambitious, but sometimes the client is not entirely convinced, sometimes the money is not enough, sometimes it's just too difficult. And sometimes we have to drop things and change things, and reduce the complexity of the project. And in that case, what is interesting is not the things that are dropped, but the ones that remain. Because if they ask: 'Can we cut this part here?', of course we are going to say: 'No'. This is one of the things we can never drop. But however this process makes you drop several aspects of the initial design bit by bit; the ones that remain are those that we think are really important.[54]

Another architect, Alain Fouraux, known among the other architects as the 'artist', provided me with a lot of information about the design process in the OMA. I held a series of interviews with him on a number of projects he has worked on.

At the age of 14, Alain Fouraux started his professional career in creative disciplines parallel to his education – radio advertising, painting, sculpture, video productions, animations and product design. Alain found a way to channel his rapidly expanding interest in the field of architecture and urban design, leading him to become one of the main concept designers at the OMA where he has been responsible for many landmark designs. He is the main designer of the Times Museum, Guangzhou, in conjunction with Rem Koolhaas.

ALAIN: I am a native Dutchman, so I really wanted to get out of Holland and start creating my own stuff. Anywhere would do. At the beginning I worked as a designer on Prada, at the start of the schematic design, and I worked in New York and San Francisco basically. And then I worked on the Astor Hotel, also at the commencement of the project. Then the LACMA, and the last competition was Amsterdam. Now we are starting the CCTV project, and I don't have so much to say about this.

(…) Certainly, the most important thing that I've learned here, and this is the thing I have to be grateful to this office for, is that it liberates you from any kind of formal language and media language. Especially since I've done so many different kinds of concepts in such a short time. I have never had problems with style or anything. If Rem asks me something, even if it is something banal, he can say: 'Look at this artist, I want to have him as building.' It's really no problem for me. I really enjoy these kinds of things. Basically there are no conventions, like material, or even formal language, and this is something that is really nice in this office. And we had this kind of period when we started to believe that we are always going in the opposite direction from intuition, so we were really experimenting with our own minds, by simply designing and thinking about how it could work. We always end up by doing something beautiful. That's really nice as compared to other offices.[55]

There were very few women in the office. Olga Aleksakova was one of them. She devoted a lot of her time to my questions and shared both moments of excitement and disappointment.

Olga Aleksakova graduated in 1998 with distinction from Delft University of Technology. She worked for 5 years at the OMA on Universal Headquarters in Los Angeles, Almere Masterplan, Cinema and shopping complex Blok 6 in Almere, Whitney Museum in New York, and LACMA Museum in Los Angeles. She was a project architect for Flick museum in Zurich, the Hermitage extension in Saint Petersburg, and Krost Masterplan for Quarter 75 in Moscow. She is currently a partner of Buromoscow.

OLGA: We often joke: we say that we have two lines like the Nike lines: OMA classic and OMA swoosh. And OMA swoosh comprises projects like PORTO, so the new line is when the form is much more expressive than the classic. Seattle is almost the end of OMA classic. And if you look at Cordoba, it's all new line. It can be a model, it can be a diagram. In the Oslo project there was a strange shape line of the site. So, we took the programme as secure and we put it on the site and created the future programme. So, that's why you always have

54 Interview with Sho, April 2002, OMA.
55 Interview with Alain, April 2002, OMA.

to go back and forth, checking repeatedly. Is it still the same diagram? Do the programme and the shape still fit together, or are they readable as separate entities? At the end you have to sell it again. And if people see that it doesn't work, they are not convinced. That was the strength of the Seattle project, because now we can explain it in three sentences, and you can argue about its aesthetics but its logic is so strong that people buy it even if they don't like the form. (…) I think that there are different ways of considering it. There is a split in the office. The older generation are more for the classic line than for the swoosh line. For example, the people from the older generation don't like Whitney, because to them it's just a shape, but I think it's so beautiful that they can't imagine it.[56]

Erez Ella was my main interviewee on the Whitney project, but he also helped greatly in getting acquainted with the office routines and I learned a lot from him.

Erez Ella is an Israeli architect who joined the OMA in 1999. As an Associate at OMA Rotterdam and OMA New York he worked on the Whitney Museum of American Art in New York, the Television Cultural Center for China Central Television (CCTV) in Beijing, the Los Angeles County Museum of Art (LACMA), Museum Plaza in Louisville, Kentucky, the Dee & Charles Wyly Theatre in Dallas, Texas and the new headquarters for Vakko in Istanbul. He is now based in New York City and is the co-founder of REX in collaboration with Joshua Prince-Ramus. In 2006 the two architects turned OMA's New York office into Ramus Ella Architects, or REX, and took over several American OMA commissions.

EREZ: The particularity of this studio is that whatever you want to do you can do it. And it is more appropriate for the design and for your ideas. For example, we have concrete materials for NATO and it was necessary to have solid and other materials. So, you use materials that you think are appropriate, and again it's like a sketch but it's a model. The sketch doesn't show everything. It shows the ideas and also the concept. While the concept models show the ideas that you want to express. (…) The computer is the worst; it takes more time. CCTV has these computer-generated models that we call renderings. It's easier to have them. For Prada it's just a model in the city, that's easier. But I wouldn't say that we don't use the computer; we use computers all the time. But we do not use computer renderings. Purely because it's more time consuming. But we also need people who know how to do it, how to use the software. So, we need to generate a completely new manpower function in the office somehow. Of course, there are people who know how to do it, but it takes more time. These things are too standard for me.[57]

Ole Scheeren was the first person Rem introduced me to and he remained my main contact person throughout the duration of my entire study. I was in regular contact with Ole, who informed me about different office events and project developments; most of my interviews were held in his glass office.

Ole Scheeren joined Rem Koolhaas and OMA in 1995 and became a partner in 2002. Since 1999 he has directed OMA's work for Prada and completed the Prada Epicenters in New York City (2001) and Los Angeles (2004). He has led numerous other projects, including the Beijing Books building, the Los Angeles County Museum of Art, the Leeum Cultural Center in Seoul, and a blueprint for Penang Island, Malaysia. He is now director of OMA Rotterdam and OMA Beijing and in charge of the office's work across Asia. As partner-in-charge of OMA's largest project to date, he is leading the design and construction of the China Central Television Station CCTV and the Television Cultural Center (TVCC) in Beijing.

OLE: We are also not an office that really designs on computers. We use computers for production and for rep-

56 Interview with Olga, October 2002, OMA.
57 Interview with Erez, November 2002, OMA.

resentational work, but not actually for the design work. We have not started to explore the numeric space. The offices that have done that have ended up with a style of blob and fluidity that I am not sure if it's the accurate answer to numeric space and vector-related descriptions of space. In that sense we are very modern, not contemporary, but very modern or a very old office, very old in our techniques and ways of working.

AY: When you said modern I was thinking about the classification of the OMA's style as super-modern style [according to NAi's classification]. What do you think about that? You are already in the history of architecture styles, and you have been labelled 'super/ultra-modern' architects.

OLE: Super-modern? This is extreme!

AY: This is bizarre because, according to Rem's writings, your work should be regarded as being situated in a non-modern rather than super-modern tradition.

OLE: [Silence] So, I am not the person who can give you an accurate answer to that. Although I would like to say one thing. I really have strong doubts as to whether the sense of the contemporary or the modern really implies anything related to the kind of stylistic judgment that is usually made. I am not actually sure why our architecture is qualified or classified as super-modern, and not as contemporary. I also wonder what would be actually qualified as contemporary in this case. And how is something like Frank Gehry's architecture more contemporary in its understanding or maybe in its usability? So, there are so many levels and layers of actually reading and describing architecture. You can go into stylistic one, into a sculptural one, into a programmatic one, into a representational one, and maybe even one of social and political awareness, one of media-related effects. And then, all these things might look slightly different. But I think what distinguishes our architecture is probably that its formal aspects are very much based on the modern vocabulary rather than, as I mentioned, this numeric vector-based, fluid and blob-like vocabulary that has developed, based on the development of computers and numeric space. At the same time, I think that the actual social or sociological, or cultural understanding of the work is, to me, by no means less contemporary than many of the things that pride themselves on a certain style that predicts contemporariness in itself.[58]

I think that we are totally non-artistic office in a certain way. I think that our approach is a much more programmatic or pragmatic one. Let's see, in the case of Whitney, the fact that it produced this very – I would prefer to call it sculptural rather than artistic – this very sculptural shape was not based on the fact that it was actually a museum, or something related to art. In a rational sense, that might have driven us away from any artistic approach. And again LACMA is a very good example, because LACMA is a very pragmatic approach, we talked about the infra-structural aspect of the project. I think that Whitney developed into this sculptural shape and object of weirdness simply because the basic givens of the project were so absurd in themselves that they necessarily produced an absurd answer that resulted in a sculptural shape, taking into account the political situation, the programme, the history. But at the same time I don't want to pretend that there would ever be a formula or a logical conclusion in architecture. I don't think that anything in architecture in that sense is truly logical, and can be derived from that, there is no clear answer.[59]

I think Seattle was also really a question of not only what is a library, but also of what is a library today in the media and communication age, how a library has to reinvent itself. It is not so much about the new, but more about the actuality of a programme and the understanding of what it

58 Interview with Ole, November 2002, OMA.
59 Interview with Ole, November 2002, OMA.

implies as a transformation. Rather than a new idea, we try to generate profound understanding of the programme or typology in the actual context now.

AY: So, it is not about designing for the future?

OLE: Yes, it is about current ideas, about actuality. There is a lot of sense of the present in every case. And at the same time I think that every project does deal with the future, because it accepts and maybe sometimes even thematizes the knowledge of an almost unpredictable future change to happen. And it questions the kind of change that can be allowed for and accommodated.[60]

Carol Patterson was the Whitney project manager and I was in regular contact with her for the Whitney project.

Carol graduated and was awarded the AIA Gold Medal at the University of California, Berkeley. She is currently Project Manager at the OMA. She was the project manager of major OMA projects such as the LACMA extension and the extension to the Whitney Museum of American Art. Previously to that she worked as a senior architect at Arup Advanced Geometry Unit and was Associate at Rogers Marvel Architects.

CAROL: I think that there is always a way of describing a project that is completely rational, even if the project itself may look not so rational. Generally they are really rational. Because you go through a period of research, we get back and everything is done. You have to do so much research before you get your point. Sometimes research may come out after the fact, because you do something, you like it, but you want to justify it or verify that what you are doing is correct. So you make a back-up and make sure that your back-up information supports the idea. So a lot of it is just a rational way of explaining something. This does not necessarily mean that someone likes this project, but it's actually incredibly reasonable in terms of what they had given us to work with. It's like 'Oh, perfect, it makes perfect sense'. But I think you need all that background information to understand why it makes so much sense. And it should

always be as clear as possible, as understandable as pos- **41**
sible in a very short way, rather then needing many
explanations.[61]

If you look at the CCTV. There were some models that
were very abstract in a way and they were meant to be
very beautiful. And they were beautiful. Even right at
the beginning the intention was to follow the technical
requirements of the competition, which meant a large-
scale and a small-scale model. And they re-inversed the
thing and they made the large scale model very abstract
and the small-scale model very detailed. Even though
the judges knew that it was probably the winning scheme,
the abstract was just too abstract and they didn't even
understand the beauty in there. Perhaps it was China
and all these politicians, but in the making of the final
model they were realistic. And again that's another way
of seducing clients with models. So, who can you seduce
with this? You can only seduce with an abstract model.
If you get through the details you start thinking about
too many angles of the thing, and that produces many
details. But to a lot of our clients, 'realistic' is the way
they can imagine something. So we need to have a balance of how you can make something beautiful and
seductive, and at the same time imaginable, feasible.[62]

Kunlé Adeyemi was one of the young architects working
in the Whitney team. He allowed me to follow his work in
slow and painstaking design operations.

Kunlé Adeyemi joined the OMA in 2002. As a Senior
Associate of OMA, he is presently in charge of several ongoing projects: the Qatar Foundation Headquarters, the
Central Library and the Strategic Studies Center, all in
the Education City in Doha, the new Headquarters tower
for the Shenzhen Stock Exchange in China, the Prada
pavilion project in South Korea and, most recently, the

60 Interview with Ole, September 2002, OMA.
61 Interview with Carol, April 2002, OMA.
62 Interview with Carol, October 2002, OMA.

4th Mainland bridge and blueprint project in Lagos, Nigeria.

KUNLÉ: Generally speaking, the more things we do, the better it is. Of course at the same time this means more resources and time consumption. I believe that, at this level of practice, this is a sort of extravagance we have right now. Otherwise we cannot move towards perfection. Because design is not exactly linear. And we have to do something new, it requires much more time. There are a lot of ways, and in the options you can find the solutions. You can find totally different objectives in the local options. Some options are so stupid and standard, but occasionally in the routine you think 'Oh, there is something interesting'. It can be applied to many things we do here, models and drawings. And we start to analyse these options and evaluate them, and come to a final result. The more you can realize, the better it is. Nothing should be wasted.[63]

AY: How do you distinguish the good models from the bad models? Which models do you consider as good?

KUNLÉ: Ohhh. I find it very difficult to say that it's a bad model, you know. You could have a model that is not really successful in illustrating a specific idea or point. Perhaps in that sense you could say that it's a bad model. But apart from that, it's difficult to justify the logic of what makes up good or bad architecture. But the good model is one that succeeds in illustrating some ideas. Perhaps everybody in the team will find some model distasteful or not very nice. And that model suddenly becomes the most important model to somebody who can see some potential in it, an idea. So, in that sense, I'm always very sensible when judging whether it's good or bad. Sometimes the things that are more grotesque or perhaps the more repugnant models may have some interesting qualities on closer inspection. It all depends on who is evaluating it and how he or she is able to explore the opportunities in the model, the resources. But of course we do have some very uninteresting models.[64]

And here is the voice of an external architect – Abji – who
came from the firm DBB (Davis Brody Bond, a New York
City based firm providing expertise in architectural planning, programming, preservation, interiors, consultative,
and collaborative services). He spent a couple of months
working on the Whitney project in OMA, Rotterdam:

AY: Do you like working at the OMA?

ABJI: Yes, yes it's nice. It's a very informal atmosphere. It's
very relaxing sometimes. And we have a lot of work.
You can't do so many things in the city of Rotterdam.
In New York there are so many things happening. You
can go out in the city; you know there are so many
things happening and you want to experience the city
culturally. Here, there is nothing. I go home and sometimes I don't have dinner like for two days, because I
work during the evenings. Everything is closed and
I don't have time to do shopping.

AY: That's how everybody works here?

ABJI: Yes, we even work in the weekends, but it's OK, It's a
good atmosphere.

AY: Do you see some important differences in the practices
of this office and your office in NYC?

ABJI: Yes, I see lots of differences. We do make models in
DBB, but we don't primarily use models as a means of
studying the impact of the design. We don't do models
every day. There will be one person that does the models
of all the ideas, you know. At the same time there are
3-D studies going on side by side. It's a parallel process;
it's not a linear process. At the OMA one stops, the other
begins, one informs the other. It's side by side. We also
do it at DBB but it's not so advanced, because our clients
are different. We also take part in competitions. The
nature of the client determines to a large extent exactly
what the process is going to look like.'

AY: There is an overproduction it seems to me [*to provoke*

---

63 Interview with Kunlé, June 2002, OMA.
64 Interview with Kunlé, September 2002, OMA.

him]. I cannot compare this to another office, but that's my impression.

ABJI: Yes, an overproduction also because of the nature of the work. Because the OMA is really looking for a higher level of theoretical input in the project. Every architect can do the project in accordance with the client's requirements. That's what the competitions are about. But OMA wants to go a step further in terms of really original ideas, pushing the local context, thinking about architecture. It is not simply about building something, the programme and the shape, but it's also about what architecture can bring culturally, it's about thinking differently. Therefore, you have to start looking exclusively at more visual production. A new concept is important, but you also have to have a lot of information to back it up, you know.[65]

Listening to these voices we can outline two distinctive features of the process at the OMA. First, invention happens in the process of 'taking models seriously', experimenting and expressing by means of models, and using a variety of other tools in original ways. The work with models is at the basis of novelty and innovation.[66] New insights and building shapes emerge from a charade of visuals and the environment in the office. It is a foam – rather than a computer – office. Second, the office 'liberates' architects from any kind of formal and media language; there are no conventions that would restrict invention.

To further understand the foam-specificity of the OMA and question the architects' attachment to models, I conducted a little test.

---

65 Interview with Abjihit, June 2002, OMA.
66 While the significance of the architectural drawing is largely discussed, the role of models in design practice has seldom been tackled in the design literature (see Akiko, 1991; Bonfilio, 2000; Porter and Neale, 2000).

Waiting for Ole, I was staring at the models scattered around when Ole entered the office, breathless from the last meeting. Without waiting for him to sit down and make himself comfortable for an interview session in the glass office, I asked a question:

AY: How many models are usually generated in the course of a project?

OLE: We obviously start with the conceptual model of the building and it can easily go until, I don't know, 30-50 models. All the models that you see here are for the same project. I mean, there are not many now, there are probably 12 models on the shelves but this is also at the point when the project has already left the office and most of these things have to disappear, so there is fairly a big quantity of things. (…) At the same time since we have so much work with this experimentation, we just decided to apply a new strategy and simply change the methods and the means by which the office works. We just had a conversation with Rem this morning and we decided not to allow any blue foam anymore in the office for a month, to substitute making with thinking and to force people to first think what they want to do instead of producing some rough quantities of trials and slowly find something that would work.[67]

This experimental 'one month without models' never happened. Was it because it appeared to be a difficult task for OMA architects to 'substitute making with thinking' and for the head architect 'to force people to first think what they want to do instead of producing some rough quantities of trials and slowly find something that would work'? Or, was it because architects simply cannot think without making, and whatever the experiment is launched, they could stick to alternative schemes of design thinking only

---

67 Interview with Ole, February, 2002.

temporarily. As the time passed, my disappointment grew as I was hoping to witness a breach of the routines in this office and to be able to recount the mechanisms of design making that a breach in everyday practice can reveal.

I questioned the architects on numerous occasions about the experimental 'one month without models'. Impatient to see it taking place and to report its results, I tested their readiness to follow the guidance of the master architect without making it a central point of discussion. I often mentioned the question in an innocent way in the middle of an interview: 'By the way, Rem and Ole are planning to conduct an experiment consisting of 'one month with-out…'. What do you think about it? I used the intention of the chief-architects to set up this 'one month without models' experiment as a way to open up both the routines of interview making and the designers' routine experiences. Alain recalls the moment of Rem's decision: 'I remember Rem was getting a little bit sick from the whole production of options and models, I think that there is a new drift to reduce models a little bit.'[68] Commenting on the experiment Carol said: 'I think it would definitely be an interesting experiment. I think some people are better in drawing, others are better in thinking with models.'[69] Just like Carol, other architects qualified the experiment as interesting and challenging, but did not engage in detailed reflection on its conditions of possibility or its eventual consequences.

To understand the use of the models in the studio, I was constantly deploying the intention of Rem and Ole to try to unravel, from their reactions, the models' role and practical meaning at the OMA. When I told Erez and Sarah about the 'one month without models' experiment, they were amazed. They said: 'It's not possible to work without models, you can have drawings and diagrams, but with the model you can visualize the thing in few seconds.'[70] They also thought that it will be more difficult for Rem to stick to the experimental protocol. Erez even argued that: 'This is almost impossible in this office. It won't happen. Because Rem always wants to see the last changes on a project fast

and only models enable him to see things in seconds. Rem   **47**
wants to see the model and where exactly we put the cool-
ing tower, for instance. It's easier with the model and you
can demonstrate everything in few seconds, much faster
than with a sketch.'[71] Olga also commented on the impos-
sibility of the office working without models: 'This studio
cannot work without models and foam. It's not possible.
Rem was just bored with a lot of blue foam pieces, and he
told us not to use blue foam, but white foam, because he
couldn't see blue foam anymore. And then, white foam
was so difficult to find in Netherlands, so we had a big
problem. And then, we had to spray the blue foam, it's
ridiculous.'[72]

Very few architects commented on the experiment as a
challenge that could have positive effects, and if it happened it would only outline one of the best qualities of the
OMA: 'Yes, why not? I think that you can always change your
approach easily, and it's just a matter of attitude. I mean,
that is also *the quality* of this office, we often change our
attitude. We were doing less research, before design began
to be more intuition-based. This new trend started with the
Porto building. And then the Astor Hotel was definitely
based mostly on scientific research.'[73]

I soon understood why this experiment couldn't take
place at the OMA in spite of the fact that Ole and Rem were
strongly committed to revolutionizing the office methods.
The architects at OMA think by making and rescaling models, by packing models in boxes and moving them to the
ground floor, by staging models for presentations, by circulating them within the networks of design. OMA architects
cannot substitute making with pure thinking.

And, here I am, an anthropologist of architecture at-

68 Interview with Alain, 17 April 2002.
69 Interview with Carol, 22 April 2002.
70 Discussion with Sarah and Erez, 10 April 2002.
71 Interview with Erez, November 2002, OMA.
72 Interview with Olga, April 2002, OMA.
73 Interview with Alain, April 2002, OMA.

tempting to answer the questions that resonated in all the architectural voices: How does the everyday making of things – mainly foam models – in an architectural office evolve into a form of making that is genuinely of a design nature? How can cutting foam, experimenting with materials and shapes, retouching an image with Photoshop or sketching things on tracing paper give rise to something admirable, something that sparks the architects, and talks back to them, something that will trouble them and consume their energy through the course of the design, something that will compel and surpass its maker? How do everyday making, experimentation and enjoyment of design develop into a specific architectural understanding of design?

Stories

From bubbles to rhythms

Foam is everywhere – on the shelves, on the floor, on the table of models, in the kitchen. 'It is very chaotic,' says Rem. I follow the work of the architects, drawing on their computers, cutting the foam on the cutter, moving models from the ground floor to the 7th floor, going back and forth between the terrace and the office spaces, the kitchen in the middle of the office, and the corridors creating transitions and obstacles for the movements of bodies crisscrossing the office in a daily working muddle. At some moments the office looks like an enormous black hole with various fragile points, horizontal layers and vertical sections that create a non-dimensional, non-localizing chaos.

At other moments it seems to be organized around a cadence, a sequence of operations, whose meticulous performance and repetition might create a tempo. Follow the movements of models and architects, boxes and drawings, material samples and plans, the nodes in their complex trajectories, their different speeds, the gestures, the various sonorities, and you will find out that what looks like chaos at the beginning is more of a rhythm, or many distinctive rhythms.

Even though the office is structured in bubbles – teams working on particular projects creating spaces that, although distinct, can mingle and overlap in a dynamic way – the architects still remain dispersed. A certain distribution according to the particular project bubble can be followed, but it is not entirely fixed and predictable. One thing that shows us the irregular dispersion of the designers is the OMA system of telephone calls. If you want to reach Erez from outside, you ring the office reception first; the receptionist then spreads a vocal message that echoes throughout the entire office: 'Erez, call the reception, please, Erez, call the reception!' As soon as the sound waves of the receptionist's voice, amplified by a loudspeaker, reach Erez in some part of the office, Erez has to find a telephone handset on any of the work tables. He calls the reception, tells the receptionist the internal number written on the handset and hangs up. And if the same telephone rings in a minute – we know Erez is traceable, he has a location in the office, far from or close to his project bubble, he has been reached. None of the architects has a fixed phone number, a landline, as they do not have permanent working places; the small procedure I have just described is needed to locate them in the office.

Pursue Shiro as he moves from Ole's glass-wall office, where a discussion over the CCTV project just took place, with a small-scale model in hand, as he passes through the kitchen to fetch a fresh coffee holding it with the other hand, balancing carefully with the two precious objects in his hands, and cautiously moving towards the table of models where other CCTV models, plans and drawings are being placed. Chase Erez coming from the terrace after a break, passing through the table of models of the Whitney project, pausing for a moment to see the last update on the project, before he goes back to his computer. Chase Olga as she cuts a piece of foam to produce a competition model of the NATO headquarters, takes it in her hands and starts dancing, still holding it up in her hands, staring at it, moving around and showing it to all randomly encountered architects from other project bubbles. The balancing Shiro, speeding Erez, and even dancing Olga don't move in a homogeneous office space-time, but according to many spaces, times and heterogeneous elements, according to numerous spatial transitions. It is only because they come back again to the table of models, to the kitchen, to the terrace, to the computer tables, to the ringing telephone handsets, that specific office places are generated.

What is the importance for OMA designers of these tiny daily trajectories between the model shop and the 7th floor, between terrace and studio, presentation plinths and drawing pads? What does it mean for a foam model to circulate, to have a life in the OMA, to be classified and stored in archives, to be rediscovered and reused? What does it mean to generate a new shape, to have a new idea, to design? All these trajectories are to be meticulously traced, all these issues are to be tackled with care instead of quickly explaining them with social factors or elucidating the meaning of architecture by appealing to the architect's individuality.

Things are flying around

Follow the designers as they work on the table of the NATO competition. The dense foam environment allows the interpretation of sensory data. The disorder, the density and intensity of the scattered foam contains conditions for manifesting the affective quality of the perceived model; it predisposes the architects to discern specific perceptive shapes. Foam models and try-outs are kept everywhere in the office because they are also material traces of the design process, holding the imprints of recent projects and design decisions, and documenting important moments in office life. Yet, the office environment is not a static and amorphous canvas of the design process. It is made by moving flows of various foam objects, material samples and visuals, whose shapes can be distinguished and materially separated from each other, thus creating an environment meant to facilitate the experiencing of the as-yet undefined building.

Though the blue foam is everywhere, nothing comes out of the blue in the OMA. 'Things are flying around,' adds Erez when describing the environment in the studio, and indeed things do circulate at a great pace in the foam environment of the office, and change places so often that it is difficult to distinguish foam from materials that get randomly enrolled in the design. The flow of things often brings a mundane object into circulation and allows it to take part in the design experimentation, helping the architect to imagine new shapes for the building-to-be. The designer moves in this environment, encounters a piece of foam or a mundane object, and this encounter often surprises her, that is, it triggers an event.

If you look carefully at images of the LACMA models you will find out that the roof of the future museum was made out of a pair of stockings. These mundane objects flooded the design process to play the role of a thin, ephemeral roof texture. Stockings were combined with metal to make a new roof for the LACMA complex.[74] The LACMA model is considered to be 'one of the best models we have ever built,' Erez announces. 'It is really good. There is a balance between details and abstraction, and between what it shows and why. So, it helps a lot for winning a competition.'[75] The architects experimented with different roof textures, trying to meet the challenge of designing a museum under a transparent roof in an attempt to accommodate art in a milieu where it will be viewed in a lively environment and at the same time will be protected from direct light and sun exposure. The roof experiment with stockings has nothing to do with the tone set by one of the masterpieces exhibited in LACMA – Rufino Tamayo's painting entitled *Woman with Black Stockings*, dating from 1969. It only aims at testing different light conditions: 'They have art from 16th and 17th century and, with the incidence of sunlight, we needed a different roof for this building; a transparent one. But this roof is very vulnerable now, it's a plastic sheet. And it doesn't have the UV value. It's not easy to control the light and the shade. It's very beautiful, but as a museum roof it's not so credible. So, we experimented with stockings to produce another roof.'[76] That is how the pair of stockings bought in Rotterdam ended on a museum roof in Los Angeles.

Another mundane object randomly encountered in the office – a bottle of Pepsi – inspired the design of the Astor Hotel in New York. Here is the story:

Alain: 'Oh, that was the advantage of not thinking. We were kind of desperate and we did a project that we really liked. It had seven towers and the client liked it so much as well. (...) And we were all so happy about it. And then they started calculating and found out that the buildings would be twice as expensive. (...) Then we began to get a bit desperate. In having to adapt our proposal, we underwent a couple of weeks of complete confusion. We decided to inverse our intuition and to create the opposite of what we were doing. It turned out to be some sort of block-like, heavyweight building as opposed to a kind of transparent needle-like building. I found a bottle of Pepsi in the office and we transformed it into a mould. Yes, ha, ha ha! We were just bored and we were just playing around.'[77]

The Astor story of invention is often told by other OMA designers: 'Alain was just gluing something with glass pieces [the Pepsi bottle] and then it became something.'[78] The plastic material used for Prada is also interpreted as being the result of 'playing around'. 'Alain took the same material but on a smaller scale, like the kitchen one, and he inserted it between the model's walls.'[79] Moreover, this little invention has reduced the production costs by thousands of dollars. Playing around with foam and mundane objects as ordinary as a bottle of Pepsi, a pair of stockings and kitchen plastic is a part of the daily design routines at the OMA. As another architect put it: 'We just engage in a kind of brainstorming session, seeking possibilities for what would look best. It's a weird start, but we want to see the shape immediately.'[80] Yet, there is no brainstorm session in the traditional sense of a collective creative technique for enhancing the quality of ideas, creating conditions for a blank brain to be sparked and stormed in order to generate an idea, which will be then modelled in foam. In fact,

---

74 As Ole says, 'What is interesting about LACMA is that it is a design of an infrastructure that can actually accommodate a museum that is yet to be invented and is meant to be constructed in the future.' (Interview with Ole, September 2002, OMA). It is also an example of ignoring the context, making it a kind of *tabula rasa* and starting from the beginning. That is a very different design technique from that applied in other OMA museum projects such as the NEWhitney museum for instance – whose interesting shape came as an answer to intricate constraints.
75 Interview with Erez, November 2002, OMA.
76 Interview with Olga, April 2002, OMA
77 Interview with Alain, April 2002, OMA.
78 Interview with Olga, April 2002, OMA
79 Interview with Olga, April 2002, OMA
80 Interview with Sho, April 2002, OMA.

we witness a different process: moving in the office, being surprised by numerous foam and mundane objects, turning around the table of models, adding new models and taking out others. There is a moment when the architect starts imagining the building. The foam in the office intensifies the sense of immediate living; models are objects of intense admiration, of thought provocation.

Making and thinking happen together and result in experimental conceptual models that are reminiscent of wicked dinosaurs. They are 'monster models', i.e., as-yet unshaped design works that contain the germs of a building-to-be. The first models are gatherings of a number of foam and non-foam pieces; later on they become gatherings of human and non-human concerns that impinge in design and confer shape upon the building. Far from being expressions of subjective energies, incorporations of insights and ideas, symbols of great leaps of imagination, they subsist as 'things'. 'Every model has one or more things. You cannot really say what is that – a composition of few things, of materials, of whatever.'[81] As such they accommodate a contested assembly of conflicting demands, restrictions to demolish, constraints of history, programme, zoning, typologies, structure and roof, mechanical and electric systems as well as a variety of human concerns – users' experiences and client's demands, all translated, transplanted into and accommodated by one entity – the model. As Ole put it: 'The model is confronted with these experiences to show how well it is able to accommodate an almost random number of things. And it is even more important to show the ability of the scheme to develop a multiplicity of qualities, although it should not pre-empt any of those. The model is rather the indication of a principle, of a potential that the building can offer.'[82]

There is also a moment when designers say: 'Let's push some foam and see what will come out of it.'[83] By working with foam, architects gain insights they might not have achieved otherwise: 'If you desperately want to find a smart idea, you go cutting foam,' argues Olga. Listen to her ex-

plaining the moment of surprise at what comes out in the
process of foam cutting:

OLGA: 'If you try desperately to find a smart idea, you go
cutting foam.'

AY: Are you telling me that you do not do a sketch or a
drawing before making the model, and that you do not
have a particular idea in mind before cutting the foam?

OLGA: 'You stop thinking, you just look at the piece of
foam and you try to make it beautiful, you cut. Sometimes you slice something, and then another thing, and
ou-u-u-p-p-p something is there. And you think: "Oh,
that's interesting"; it's there. Of course we always have
a sense of what Rem would like, but when you cut you
no longer know what you like in advance.'[84]

Plunging into the nebulous foam, cutting and shaping it,
allows architects a positive interaction with, and observation of, models and other foam try-outs, which permits
them to compare the slow process of shaping with the surprise and even shock from the shape that emerges in front
of their eyes. If the foam presented itself to Olga as an
amorphous milieu a few moments ago, the architect could
feel the impact of foam's sudden objectivity on her, of
abrupt encounter, in the instant of surprise; it strikes and
embraces a shape. The designer experiences the aesthetic
moment, her 'ou-u-u-p-p-p' moment when her ideas cease
to be mere ideas and become the shared significance of
objects. The designer thinks as she works, her thought
springs out of the object more immediately.[85] Caught in a
game of contrast between what the architect expects to
discover and what emerges in front of her, the model surprises as it discloses the germs of a new idea.

Look at Victoria cutting foam with the foam-cutter:

81 Interview with Erez, November 2002, OMA.
82 Interview with Ole, September 2002, OMA.
83 Interview with Erez, November 2002, OMA.
84 Interview with Olga, April 2002, OMA.
85 This observation contradicts the traditional understanding of design as a process
of transferring ideas from the designer's mind to a physical form (see Porter, 1979).

58 she adjusts her movements according to the different speeds of the instrument; she pushes the regulator button, adjusts the scale, guides the piece of foam to the edge of the burning heat, thus eliminating parts of the foam's mass by burning its texture. 'It gets hot, and it burns and cuts the material; that's why it smells,' says Shiro while cutting foam on the adjacent table. While curving the foam, architects can modulate and modify the shapes according to the manual speed, the scaling of the foam, the technical performance of the instrument, the intensity of the smell of the burnt material. The thinking about the size and the proportions of the model is rooted in the foam-cutter. Allowing changes in the angle of cutting and the speed with which one cuts, this technique permits architects to generate specific shapes that cannot be produced with other modelling techniques.

While manipulating foam, Shiro and Victoria feel that they are positioned inside the material, producing its curves and shapes: 'You have a mass, the matter is there, and it is transformed.' It is a crafting process of matter transformation: they fight with the foam, adapt their postures to its requirements, leave their imprints in its texture. Foam allows them to generate shapes that cannot be produced with other materials. As Olga explains, this is because 'you can test things with foam much more quickly'. Foam is more flexible than resin, metal and wood – materials usually used for presentational models by a professional model-maker.[86] It is soft, direct and versatile, easy to shape 'once you get your hands on the foam-cutter'. Foam guides the way designers 'cut a straight line,' argues Shiro, and allows more shaping, boxing and enclosing of things. Thus, architects delegate to the material the power to enfold, to the extent that the foam can begin to dominate the model-maker at a given moment, and the 'knowing architect' loses mastery over the building he is striving to understand. Foam cutting is the perfect medium for rapid thinking, allowing them to imagine the new shape in the moment of cutting instead of anticipating in advance.

Engaging in communication with foam as a direct and
very interactive material, architects feel the effect of every
new model they make. Slicing and manipulating the foam,
they are not completely aware of what exactly they are
doing and where their work is going. Nevertheless, they
experience each particular effect of every action in relation
to the whole that is being produced. Thus, architects discover what they are doing in the course of doing it. The
as-yet undefined building coerces the architects and the
matter guides them to define it. Designers are never alone
in the creative process; they are constantly interrogated,
guided and directed by the design work, exploring the
various paths that lead towards its concrete presence. One
cannot separate the designers' actions from the emergence
of a shape, nor their thoughts and associations from the
visual and tactile experience in the process of moving
according to many foam transitions, the movement from
the shape that is being felt. The shape of the building-to-be
derives from a concrete experience of the office environment and the concrete experience of model making, rather
than from a series of mental operations. It emerges for the
designer who perceives it *in concreto* as an object of investigation from a large number of foam works. The reality
of design consists of following the matter as it unfolds,
accepting its surprises, traces of movements and tactile
resistances. Every move in the model shop, with AutoCAD,
with the foam-cutter and on the drawing board, as well as
every move in the foam office environment, shapes the
perceptive matter of a building-to-be, as a movement, as a
new disposition.

---

86 I would like to distinguish between 'presentation models' and 'working models'.
This distinction is not made in the practices of designers at the OMA. Presentational
models – which contain the final fully developed concepts – are rarely produced
by OMA. Whenever they need to make them, they call them presentation models
to distinguish them from the numerous study and experimental models, which are
always to some extent presentation models as well in this practice.

Watch Olga as she is seized by something unexpected: she starts straying in the office with the new NATO model in her hands. Is there a design idea that precedes the shape we see as we follow Olga in her excited dance through the office, showing the model that holds the idea to all the architects from other project bubbles? No, no one can claim there is an abstract idea that first appears in the creator's mind, and is later embedded, incorporated, materialized in a shape. The idea emerges as inseparable from sensible matter; it has an objective locus. It arrives as an 'ou-u-u-p-p-p' moment in the process of cutting and shaping the foam, making mistakes and experimenting with different materials. With every move of Olga's hands cutting the foam, a shape gradually emerges; the 'monster model' moves towards the concreteness of a building-to-be. It is to become actual, intense and accomplished. It is only because foam, its folds, its bulky mass, the smell around the cutting machines are all entirely devoted to the new shape that it occurs, it exists. The meaning, the subjective, the symbolic emerges with and is inseparable from the material, the real, the objective. There are no distinctive ways of grasping an architectural object, i.e., through its intrinsic materiality or through its more aesthetic or 'symbolic' aspects. The materiality of every piece of foam kept in the office, of every 'monster model', generates meaning and changes the shape of the building-to-be.

Watch Olga staring at the model at a moment she is seized by its new shape, she starts 'dancing' with it in her hands, showing it to all the architects in the office, moving with it, holding it high but still staring at the model with admiration – that is, at the moment of seizing the model and moving with it, she feels the quality of a shape of a building-to-be. There is something mystic in design that surprises the maker, that makes her stand and stroll and dance in the space with the model in her hands. There is some sort of energy in the 'monster model'.[87] In the process of questioning it and responding to its demands and profound appeals, the designer becomes a 'victim' of the building-in-the-making. At any moment in the design, this piece of foam, this 'monster model' tells her 'I am here, but there is more to be done'. Olga is concerned with the model in her hands, troubled or passionate about it. As Ole says: 'If you look at the models we produce you can see that there is a certain amount of passion in each one of them, in different ways.'[88] Disturbed, worried, surprised, obsessed and used by it, she strives to find forces to respond to the specific requests of the design work – a blind dancer calling out to the appeals of the model in her hands.

Watch the model catching attention, being touched and transformed by the many designers' hands, slowly gaining an intense presence – all these little moves cannot be explained with the simple concepts of creation, of progressive realization of a project. Rather, the uneven model arises in a moment of invention, of instatement, a moment of acceptance and acknowledgement of the existing recollection of elements. It happens, it imposes itself in the office environment, inflicts, compels, and intrudes in the office rhythm – it is not planned and then constructed. What we witness as we follow Olga dancing, seizing the model and letting herself be seized, is the full breadth of the building-to-be. Far from being the powerful master of this process, immersed into a world of contingences, the designer helps a building happen. This is the concrete reality of design process. The building appears first as a perceptual object which embraces a shape; that means, engaging in ontology. Its unformed matter attests the actuality of perception and triggers awareness of the perceived shape.

Can we describe the trajectory traced by a piece of shapeless foam on the way to a shaped model or outline the trajectory of a model on the way to the final building without embracing an existing theoretical understanding

87 Etienne Souriau called this kind of quasi-spiritual force of the design work 'the angel of the work' (Souriau, 1956, pp. 14).
88 Interview with Ole, November 2002, OMA.

of design as realization, construction, creation or planning – all those concepts with which design has so often been described? When we follow Olga cutting and working with foam, slowly, painstakingly, until a shape emerges, we do not simply witness the progressive passage from shapeless matter to distinctive form, to reality; we do not naively believe in the realization of a project. Watch Olga, Shiro and Victoria cutting and sticking pieces of foam together and experimenting with materials. There is no gradual progression to reality, no realization of a previously conceived plan, but vertiginous hesitation, tentative moves, mistakes, miscalculated gestures, fundamental meandering, dancing. A hesitant maker, a 'monster model' that calls back its maker and demands completion, and the mystery that accompanies this process – all these elements trace a tentative trajectory, the complete opposite of a project. In the trajectory, there is no finality, but a state of incompleteness. As Ole argues: 'The process of interpretation and translation is one, and design is one that only stops when the building is finished. And sometimes it's not even there, because the building keeps on changing. I don't think there is a process where you can remove it entirely from the architect and pretend: "that was it".'[89] Designing, as witnessed in this short story, is not about projecting in a sense that something launches a new design work and throws it forward, and finds it again in the moment of accomplishment. In the project there is a beginning and an end, A and B, but the experience contingent to the process of making is neglected or rarely recounted – an experience that is so important in the design work achieving a concrete existence. Yet, in the course of what designers call 'projects', there are numerous design trajectories that account for the experience of designers in their struggles and achievements in a world of things. They constitute the nature of design.

Now, after following designers throughout model-making, can you still think of architecture as an art whose ideas are wrought out in highly technical thought like that of mathematics, or as the incorporation of symbols as an expression of abstract thought? Architectural meanings, many critics and theorists denote, are inaccessible to sense because of their spiritual and universal character.[90] But follow Shiro and Victoria cutting the foam, follow Olga seized by a model shape, and you will witness that the work with models in the OMA makes architecture a mode of activity that is charged with meaning which is capable of immediate enjoyment; it often resides in the sensible surface of things, of models. This is what makes design a complete experience of making and perceiving.

---

89 Interview with Ole, November 2002, OMA.
90 See Jencks and Baird, 1969; Venturi and Scott Brown, 2004.

Back to the office

One morning as I was chatting to Erez and hanging around the Whitney table of models, two big boxes arrived. 'The models of Guangzhou[91] are back,' said Kunlé. 'Back from where,' I asked? 'From the ground floor,' said Kunlé. 'When did they go there and why? Why are they coming back to the office, now?' All these questions lingered in my mind as I watched the architects unpacking the boxes. I became intrigued by the different circuits in a model's trajectory.

Every time I entered the 7th-floor space of the OMA everything was different: the arrangement of the tables had been changed, the people working in the project bubbles had rotated, the entire organization of the space was different. Every day I inspected the working tables of models. Kunlé told me: 'By Monday, you will probably not see half of the things you see today. Half of what we have on the table tomorrow will be totally different.'[92] Foam models have their own modes of existence in the office, their own trajectories. They are restless travellers. They are not randomly dispersed in the office, but are all kept in particular arrangements – tables of models, shelves with models, boxes full of models, books full of images of models. Designed on the tables allocated to a particular project where designers are grouped – 'the table of Whitney', 'the Porto table', 'the Seattle table', they rarely remain in the remits of the space belonging to the project bubble; they circulate in spaces, transcending the single existence of a project and overspilling the limited project boundaries. They circulate 'up-and-down' and 'in-and-out' of the office. Let us follow the trajectory of models in the office environment as they move from one material arrangement to another, and trace their metamorphoses.

Believing as they did, that there is 'something in a model', architects from the OMA act in a meaningful foam environment that can talk back to them and can act upon them as seen in the previous story that I called 'The Dance'. We can think of the foam environment of the OMA as a sort of flexible organic tissue that keeps a design project moving across tools, architects and existing foam solutions. Erez explains that they 'are not throwing models away, because sometimes there is something in a small model, and after two weeks or two months you can look at the model again, and you can see that this thing is good. And therefore we keep all the models, and when the project or the competition is finished, we just put them in boxes, archiving and putting everything down in the basement. In the basement you can find all the models, very old models. And some of the really good ones are presented at small exhibitions.'[93]

We can now recollect what happened to the models of the Guangzhou Opera House project. They stood as a material arrangement on a table of models for a while. As soon as the project was put on hold by the client, the models were packed into boxes and were transported to the ground floor. Then they were stored in the office archives and probably spent years there until they reappeared on the office tables and were dispersed all over the 7th-floor space. Archiving the models allowed architects to keep the traces of creativity for a longer period of time; de-archiving them meant they could rediscover those traces of design inventions that time had left intact. And if the models are back to the office, it means the Guangzhou project has been recently revised and new design work has been commissioned.

'Rem is very angry when we throw away models. So, we

91 Guangzhou Opera House, Guangzhou, China, 2002; Competition for Guangzhou Opera House. In 2002 the designers at OMA were working on the competition models, but Zaha Hadid won the project and she is now building it in China.
92 Interview with Kunlé, September 2002.
93 Interview with Erez, April 2002

keep *every* piece of foam. The whole production is totally self-reflexive. And it's about history, as well.'[94]

Every piece of foam? I doubt it. Had they kept every piece of foam they produced for the Guangzhou project, the office would have been flooded with foam that morning. 'Well, only the good ones,' Olga corrects herself. Indeed, only four boxes arrived in the office and were carefully opened by the architects. They followed the inventory list in the box and staged them on an empty table – the 'Guangzhou table' where the 'Guangzhou bubble' of OMA designers will be spending their days and nights.

At the same time as the models of Guangzhou reappeared in the office, the competition models for the NATO headquarters had to vanish, as the project had been unsuccessful. They were so carefully taken care of that Erez and Gabriela spent two whole days classifying the models and placing them in boxes. They explain me that Thalita is responsible for the archives. But she was nor around that day. Usually they give her the models and she puts them into boxes. This makes sense; why would a skilful designer like Erez spend two entire days packing up models into boxes? But I could not understand how Thalita, who is not an architect, could do the archiving of those models she has never worked with and how she could produce an archive of a project she vaguely knows. 'It doesn't matter,' Olga reassures me. 'She puts everything in the archives; every page is described. And you can find everything inside.'[95]

As soon as 'a project is back to the office', as OMA designers like to say, Thalita will find the boxes for them and she will bring the boxes that provide enough design works to fill the working tables. A number of projects came back to the office when I was working there: the Korean project, the 'Age' project, the Oslo project. Empty tables were named after the projects and were filled with life that swam out of the archive boxes; these tables play an important role as they gather the team and re-enact further design actions.

Put in boxes, numbered and transformed in catalogues,

all good models and try-outs are stored for the moment at which they re-enter the office circuits of design. That is why models are not thrown away. The two moves of archiving and de-archiving the models point to a very specific feature of the design process – reversibility. Archiving means putting on hold, temporarily freezing the potentials of models to induce new design shapes; de-archiving means re-engaging in the flows of things in the office, re-engaging into the networks of design. That is also an important up-and-down trajectory of the models. Going down to the basement means for models entering history, in a temporary or more durable way, whereas going up to the 7th floor means re-entering the circuits of design, coming back to actuality.

Another important up and down move in the models' trajectory is conditioned by the location of the model shop. The models go up and down many times, *up* meaning again in the office, *down* meaning the 1st floor this time, where the special model shop is located. The conceptual models initially emerge on the table of models in the 7th-floor office space but, to refine a model, designers then go down on the 1st floor to work with the special machines in the model shop. The architects explain that five years ago the model shop was in the office on the 7th floor and there was much more connection between the model shop and the other design spaces. According to Olga, a disconnection happened when the model shop was moved to the first floor:

OLGA: Because you don't want to go downstairs, and you take what ever is here and you spray things. The practice of spraying things also started when the model shop moved downstairs. I think I belong to one of the last generations who can use the milling machines. But they don't use these machines any more. The skill has been lost.

94 Interview with Olga, April 2002, OMA.
95 Interview with Olga, October 2002, OMA.

AY: Why was the model shop moved?

OLGA: Five years ago the model shop was in Rem's office. But the office was small and the model shop was in the middle of the 7th floor. And then, when the Prada project started, the office grew and we had two containers in the parking garage; but if you work in the parking garage nobody ever sees you. And then, they moved it downstairs, and now it's underused.[96]

That is how the modelling practice was incorporated into the different project bubbles, and the foam cutters landed on many office tables; modelling became an integral part of design at the OMA. The location of the model shop changed the trajectory of the model entirely. Whereas the model used to travel between the different office spaces on the 7th floor, only in a horizontal direction, in-and-out of the model shop until the model had been refined and the concept was determined, the relocation of the model shop meant that the model had to be taken down to the model shop to be transformed and refined, and up again to the office. Whenever models travel up and down to the archives, they are simply packed and unpacked and rarely get transformed. Yet, whenever they travel up and down between the office (7th floor) and the model shop (1st floor), they always get transformed; the travel brings them new modifications; you can literally see the model's metamorphoses in the gradual up-and-down moves as you bump into an architect holding a model in hands on the steep staircase connecting the floors. But whenever models travel horizontally to go out of the office and come back to it, the in-and-out trajectory brings them more alternations than they can gain in any internal up-and-down move. Models go to competitions and linger on the tables of juries and committees, planning commissions, and professional model-makers. They travel to the competition venue together with plans and other visuals. 'Maybe the models are the most memorable things; and the thing that the public connects to most of our buildings,' says Ole.[97]

Most of the OMA final models are made in the office.

For instance, the models of the NEWhitney and the LACMA were all made in-house. But when the office needs a nice final presentational model for an important competition or exhibition, the foam models are sent to the workshop of Vincent de Rijk, a professional model-maker. Contrary to what might be expected, the model that enters the workshop of Vincent and the model that comes out of it could be quite different. 'Vincent is the one who injects perhaps even more subjective qualities into things and that is why we were led to work with him,'[98] argues Ole. Vincent does not simply follow the instructions of the architects on how to produce the final model, completing a simple technical task. Known for his experimental style, he rather tries to interpret the design and generate new creative solutions. In his workshop, the blue foam model made by OMA is subjected to further experiments with a variety of techniques.

EREZ: Vincent is really good. And he is really good because he thinks. He knows that nothing is really determined, nothing is really said. So, he can also imagine things for the building, and that's good.

AY: Are there any important differences between the techniques that Vincent uses as a professional model-maker and your techniques?

EREZ: Definitely, yes. But what is nice about Vincent is that he never does anything by means of one technique. He never says 'OK, that's my technique, and I will do it in that way'. He is very good at lots of techniques and it's even better that he manages to combine all those techniques. So, that's why Rem also likes him, because he manages to discuss with him and with us as a team what would be the most appropriate technique for a model. The combination of really precise things and handmade things is the nice thing about him.[99]

---

96 Interview with Olga, October 2002, OMA.
97 Interview with Ole, April 2002, OMA.
98 Interview with Ole, November 2002, OMA.

In Vincent's workshop, models can be made with materials that cannot be seen at the OMA. Those materials require heavy machines and special equipment, which could make the model-making process quite slow. And time is what designers at the OMA are often lacking. 'A laser cutter for example is very precise for a drawing and it cuts exactly where the lines of the drawings are, but we don't have a laser cutter here at the OMA,'[100] explains Carol. The time a model spends in Vincent's workshop is precious as it allows the model to gain valuable new properties that cannot be acquired with the quick techniques of foam cutting at the OMA. Thus, every moment in the model trajectory endows it with new qualities, enriches it and transforms it; every translation modifies it and allows it to gain new properties as an engaging perceptive object. Models change in a similar way in their in-and-out trajectories between the office and the client's headquarters or the planning commission, when they meet the city mayor or a group of proto-users. In such cases, what might change the model and trigger design transformations is not the heavy machines but the serious concerns of all those involved in the project.[101]

If we keep on following the model in its horizontal travels within the OMA premises, we will find out that models also often take a rest on the table of models, on the shelves of the bookcases, sharing the space with material samples and archives, in the presentational concept books, in the archival boxes, in office presentations, in the office kitchen, in the archive drawers. All these material arrangements present a choice of visuals, not as anaesthetized and static documentation of the stages of architectural accomplishments but rather as tentative collections of 'working objects'. As such, they might provide a very specific focus for a broad scope of concepts and serve the cause of diffusion of architectural knowledge in the office.[102] They are not simple places of rest for models and images; instead, these arrangements are meant to re-enact the building and its life through a series of events.

Let us look at two of these arrangements – the tables

and the books. When concentrated on the tables, the models retain their traces of design insights and experimental scenarios.

'The models are kept on the table, because we can use some of them again and because we also need to refer to them. We have tested a scenario and it didn't work, that's the result. But we kept it. Even the models we have here on the table – and there are hundreds of models or more – still do not illustrate the full potential or all the possibilities that we could have realized. Because we have tested one issue, one scenario, it doesn't entirely eliminate a particular possibility. We shouldn't stop exploring in that direction and simply test another scenario because it may work differently there. So, what we are trying to do is not to eliminate the impossibilities. We try to keep a large range of starting points of view open, so to speak.'[103]

The table sustains the multiplicity of models. Taking into account the rapidity of changes in the design process, architects need to keep all material traces of design experimentation to remember the different scenarios that have been tested, the possibilities and directions already explored. The abandoned and rejected projects are also kept as prospective steps to successful design. Outlining the material trajectory of a project, the table makes it traceable. Every model brings an idea and embodies a new meaning. As such, the table is the material locus of design ideas. Accommodating a number of points of view and a vast range of possibilities, the table is the material brain of

99 Interview with Erez, November 2002, OMA.

100 Interview with Carol, October 2002, OMA.

101 On the particular process of circulation and feedback which the Whitney project received in the process of presenting and discussing the models with various branches of the public, see Yaneva, 2009, chapter 4.

102 I have shown elsewhere that architects pragmatically approach a building as knowable through the various practices of image-making and model-making. In cutting the foam, retouching image edges and correcting the representations on the screen, architects are not only engaged in a struggle to erase uncontrolled and disordered subjectivities; in this process, they also gain new knowledge that is not graspable otherwise (Yaneva, 2009).

103 Interview with Kunlé, September 2002, OMA.

the designers. It reminds OMA designers that 'they cannot create an intelligent scheme out of the blue'. When a key experiment is being conducted or a significant brainstorm session is being carried out, the table of models also serves as an important organizational node of the project-bubble activities. If architects want to 'make a building exist for everyone in the office, they ask everybody to put a proposal on the table overnight'.[104] Thus, the table acts as the main co-ordination point of the particular design task; it guides and redistributes the actions.

Another material arrangement of import for the model trajectory is the concept book which summarizes the project, promotes a moment of deceleration in the course of the design, and allows evaluation of the effects of design moves.

'At one point there is a stop in the process, and you collect the materials. Again you evaluate the project, and you try to sort it in a different way. And it just makes the project and your argument shorter. So, it's important, because in a way it forces you to stop, look at the project in a different manner, and evaluate it again. (...) Even after the deadline, when you look at the project book it's different. It's like the Guangzhou Opera project. We did this project, we were into it, we liked it and everything was good. And now the project is back and when I look at the book suddenly I have criticism, and I believe some of the things could have been done differently. And of course, if this project goes on, I know how to think about it differently.'[105]

Like the tables of models, the books are summaries of the design steps that make the material trajectory of a project traceable. They keep some traces of exploration, and present the results of design experimentation. Like the tables they allow the designers *to go back* and rethink the design moves previously made. They are easy to review as the entire information is collected at one place and in one format. In some cases, the books are produced not simply to inform the design process but also to inform the different groups that take part in design – clients, neighbours, possible users. For the Whitney project for example, there were several types of books of different formats for the groups of actors to whom the project was presented. The book takes the form of a brochure when architects distribute it after a public presentation, but it can have a completely different content if it is to be distributed at a meeting of the Landmark Commission. Underpinning other forms of architectural visualization, the material arrangements on the tables and in the books define the 'working objects' of architecture, and, at the same time, cultivate the office approach. They also train the architects, who are running back and forward, moving across and circulating around the tables or with the books in their hands.

As material arrangements, both the tables of models and the concept books offer a rare glimpse of design in the making. They are intended to serve the immediate practices of design. Their role is performative: not passive illustrations of projects or urban concepts, or instantaneous responses to a competition or a client's brief, but *organizational devices* used to enact further design moves, to train the younger architects and to inform the invited viewers, to teach them how to think architecturally, to encourage them to act accordingly. They provide a 'how-to' guide to design practice. Through their reiterative tutorial performance, new knowledge is gained and communicated among architects in the office and visitors.

Let us have a closer look at the visuals in a typical concept book by OMA.[106] Far from being back-boxed, aesthetically polished illustrations attesting to stabilized epistemic objects and certain knowledge, the visuals are presented in the book as dynamic cognitive objects, tentative and open, having a crucial performative impact on design practice. They offer no signs of big ideas or great leaps of imagination, but traces of executive doing, of design investigations.

---

104 Interview with Alain, April 2002, OMA.
105 Interview with Erez, November 2002, OMA.
106 To see the concept book of the Seattle Public Library for instance, please visit http://www.spl.org/cen_conceptbook/page2.htm.

The concept book depicts the experimental situations that make a model possible, and deliberately expose the relationship of that model with a variety of context-making factors. The model on these images is reminiscent to a human model sitting for and performing in the studio of a painter. Very often, the setting in which models are produced is not stripped away from the images – that theatrical quasi-technical setting is an integral part of the design events in the process of model-making. The visuals do not hide the awkward events, the brute materials, the unpolished and uncompleted surfaces, bur rather expose them as a part of office life. A number of images 'report' on the work in the studio and show designers in action. A model – and even the building – is rarely detached from the studio situation of its production, from the site of experimentation and previous enactments of the building-to-be. The building emerges first as a studio affair, as a genuine OMA production. Rather than presenting the main building's concepts and its big ideas, a concept book made by OMA restages moments of office life on its pages and re-enacts the main design events that made this building possible.

The OMA is treated in the books and the tables of models as a world that is to be re-enacted with the help of the designers. It is because the actual process of design is a combination of movements and changes, disjunctions and culminations, breaks and reunions, that the model trajectories up and down in the office and in and out of the office are capable of generating new design qualities. There is no stable design concept that travels without transformations, embodying the big insights of a 'creator' or reflecting cultural and social influences; instead, there are sinuous tentative trajectories of a restless traveller gaining meaning in the process of travelling. In this design experience, studio affairs replace the social affairs; they generate the content.[107]

---

107 On the capacity of different OMA projects to generate multiple contents, see Koolhaas et al., 1995, OMA and Koolhaas, 2004.

On a September afternoon in 2002 I had arranged to meet Erez for an interview. We decided to meet downstairs on the 1st floor – the only place we could have a discussion uninterrupted by other designers or project emergencies. Ole's glass office was another quiet space for uninterrupted discussions, but it was occupied at the time. I somehow preferred also the 1st-floor interviews because as soon as I entered its tranquil and well-organized spaces, rhythmically ordered by better arranged tables of models, I was immediately transported to the office future, an immediate future. I liked spending time on the ground floor where the busy model shop opened to a larger quasi-exhibition space, where Rem used to begin his guided tours of the office. I also remember Rem showing me around on my first visit to the OMA, and he was especially proud of some of the models you can only view in this space: some Prada experiments with sponge[108] and the huge models of buildings in construction like Porto or Seattle. I remember Rem calling the Prada sponge samples 'the material of modernity'. What I also recall is the strangeness of the material and Rem's pride. Sometimes, tired of the busy-bee rhythm of the 7th floor, I simply retired to the 1st floor to contemplate these models.

And, here was Erez, seated next to the Seattle model, feeling comfortable to be in the limelight of the interview and sharing the silent space with the models: he, like myself secretly admired most of them.

'This is a model made in 1999, it's a very conceptual thing. But you can see that these diamonds are here, it's a mesh. And they stayed until the building began to be constructed; so, this material remained throughout the process. At one point we tried some fabrics, and they stayed all the

108 Prada Sponge, Los Angeles, USA, 2004; Research and development of foam material in the use of Prada Epicenter store; built.

way on the model too. Another good example of this could be Prada; you see this material, sponge, over there [he points to the sponge samples]. So the Prada sponge at the beginning was a small model in sponge, which they tried to imitate. Chris worked quite a lot to develop the material that would really imitate it and present the same qualities and the same appearance. And eventually they managed to do it. It came from the model, almost in a direct line to the final thing.'[109]

The connection between the so-called 'diamonds' on the Seattle model and the diamond seismic system of the building-under-construction puzzled me for a while. I wanted to understand it. Erez and I looked at the Seattle diamonds together: 'Very often there is a direct connection between the material of the model and the material of the building,' states Erez. It is a literal one: 'If for instance the model has a wire mesh operating copper bottom, it's about taking that literally.'[110]

To understand how direct this connection can be, to witness how exactly the mesh of the Seattle model became a material used for the building and how the sponge as 'the material of modernity' was obtained for Prada, I shall first guide you through some related stories of material invention within the OMA practice.

Numerous stories of design at the OMA emphasize how important the techniques of model-making are for the shape of a building. Olga tells me, for instance, that a prevailing story in the office is the one about how the use of Perspex in model-making changed the world of architecture. Later I understood that it was the OMA version of this story that excited most designers at work, namely, how the foam-cutter is an invention as important as Perspex, an invention capable of changing the face of architecture. Once the transparent and easy to manipulate Perspex began to be used for models, this changed the face of the final buildings, claim OMA architects. The Perspex models 'show at one glance the outside and the inside'.[111] It also anticipated buildings with such properties. In the same way, the foam-cutter, its angle, its speed, allow OMA designers to produce curved and innovative building shapes. This particular technique triggers changes in the building design. Erez quotes another example of how the modelling guides the building design.

EREZ: The technique of modelling influences the design. If you build a square building, it's easier to build it out of foam. For example, the Guangzhou Opera House has a super-weird shape, it's a folding surface. Building this folding surface was really, really hard. So, when we develop the technique of building the model, it influences the design, because it never turns out the way you thought it would be. Then, if it's nicer it will influence the design. If it's not, you can abandon it and move on to another technique because you don't manage 'to establish beauty' as Rem says. So, it's not beautiful at first sight.

AY: And how did you manage to build it?

EREZ: We built an extension to the foam-cutter and we placed two guides on the sides for the foam with one wire. We really worked very hard, but we only obtained three models from it. Because we just couldn't build it. At that point we constructed it on the computer, and the final model was built from the 3-D computer file. Some outsourcing guy built it for us on the computer because we couldn't. Again it's time and knowledge. We can do it. But in the process in which the office works we need to produce something new for tomorrow morning, so to speak. So, we cannot spend three days building a model.[112]

There is a variety of elements that are to be taken into consideration in the making of a new model or shape: the restrictions of the site, the clients' fears, the programme requirements, the small budget, the community protests

109 Interview with Erez, November 2002, OMA.
110 Interview with Carol, October 2002, OMA.
111 Interview with Olga, October 2002, OMA.
112 Interview with Erez, November 2002, OMA.

against the design, the protected buildings, the zoning filling, the neighbours' vulnerability, etc. This list can be extended according to the specificity of each project and its destination. Yet, what remains a common feature of all buildings-to-come is that they are all 'things', i.e., contested assemblies of contradictory issues. Looking at design practice, we should add another aspect that would make the 'thingly' nature of a building easier to comprehend.[113] There are *studio events* related to the particular performance of a design object, or the substantiation of a property of an object in time. They are embedded in the process of using particular modelling techniques or in experimentation with materials and shapes. These singular events often point to the intensity of design life at the OMA. The fact that the materiality of Perspex or the specific use of the foam-cutter has a certain impact on the building's shape cannot to be doubted. Yet, the importance of these singular events for the building-to-be has not been entirely accounted for. Can a model fully predict in advance what the building-to-be will look like? Can architects be completely prepared for the building-to-come? Can the building faithfully follow its models? Both models and buildings travel and undergo changes in this process. In their attempts to move towards each other, to bring life into the studio and to re-enact it, the tentative moves of the two travellers trace a twisting trajectory interrupted or guided by studio events.

While the foam is still blue

Sitting in front of Erez that afternoon in the interview, sharing the space only with the model of the Seattle Library, I thought about the differences between the colour perception of the two office spaces. If the 7th-floor open-plan space were to be defined in colour, that would definitely be blue because of the blue foam predominantly used by the OMA. As you go downward the 1st floor, you start thinking about design in many other different colours. Why is that?

'The blue foam means that you do not have definition, it's going to be blue foam or metal and copper, maybe. So,

that's how it could then be developed. We had three models at the beginning, they were all in foam; but they were
painted – one was concrete and we sanded it until it looked
like a concrete block. One was of glass and we made a pattern on it. One was made of foam, but was a structural
model, so it had more transverse bars. And so those three
were meant to be three kinds of representations. These
models say: 'it could be concrete, it could be glass, it could
be steel. Which one do you want?' The concrete was the
more abstract and the more interesting in relationship to
the project.'[114]

Thus, we learned from Carol that blue stands for the
not-yet-defined materiality of the building-to-be. On the
one hand, the model can *represent* existing or intended
materials – steel, concrete, glass. These are all materials
that are to be taken from the catalogues. They are known
and predictable. To make a model that would represent
one of those materials would merely require simulating
their texture or form on the model. Architects would simply say: 'ok we would like to have it in copper', and they
will try to *imitate* the copper on the model. That is how
architects at the oma and architects from other practices
often work. On the other hand, in the process of office
experimentation, some new materials and material effects
can be obtained. In that case, 'architects build a scale model
to look for new materials'. The material comes as a result
of a studio event. And that is something so distinctive for
the oma.

'Sometimes we use some materials of which we are not
quite sure of how they work. We just find them attractive
and we use them on the model, and then we start developing that material. Then we call people and we discuss how
we can actually achieve this sort of effect. Sometimes we
just use a material that really does not exist. It may become
so interesting that we say "ok, it looks really nice, but how

113 On the 'thingly' nature of buildings see Latour and Yaneva 2008.
114 Interview with Carol, October 2002, OMA.

can we achieve this in reality?" That's why a lot of things are developed in the office. Some offices simply apply existing materials. Of course it's easier to use materials from the shelf, from the catalogue, but we can't be on the cutting edge if we do that. So, we develop our own materials, we develop new structures.'[115]

The experimental effect achieved on the model is to be repeated and reproduced at building level. Take the Flick house[116] for instance. At the beginning, designers constructed a blue model and they had difficulty in considering how to make 'a material that will give the same transparent light that was seen in the model'.[117] Another example is the model of the NATO headquarters. 'When we did these small lines,' explains Erez, 'it was just an experiment with the model technique. Then we tried to imitate this quality of the façade; you see it over there. So, to design the real façade we tried to imitate the façade effect we first achieved on the model.' I wondered how this effect was obtained. Could it possibly be merely skilful use of the foam-cutter, or something else? Erez replied quickly: 'This was all done with the foam-cutter, you just do a lot of stripes, and that's all.'[118] The models test true effects, as Ole describes this process. In that sense OMA models are realistic: 'We do try to test a lot of things on models with the sense of realism, which obviously still implies different degrees of abstraction, but it really also comes down to your experience, and to your ability to learn from these things.'[119] Thus, when these randomly and locally achieved effects in the concrete situation of model experimentation, as seen on the Flick and the NATO models, are to be repeated and reproduced, slowly and gradually merging into a novel material, a new tentative design trajectory is triggered. If we follow it for a while, we are certainly able to witness how a studio event plays a part in generating the reality of a building-to-be.

A material that compels the designer can easily create a studio event. 'We work with different models, and when we try to finish one we put some materials on it. We do not look at the catalogue. Instead of going outside and finding a good material, we first look at our own. If something is compelling and looks good … you can look for up to six months for some materials that simulate whatever you put into the model. It always goes from the model to the catalogue and not the other way around.'[120]

The fact that designers at the OMA refuse to use the catalogue of existing materials, preferring to pick and make their own materials *in situ*, shows the extent to which the dense foam environment provides a creative milieu for a proactive design process. It allows different materials to stimulate the makers and to involve them in model-making and experimentation. What follows is a 'let's do it' moment, which architects often recall in these stories of invention, especially for the emblematic Prada sponge. Erez tells the story: 'Somebody just hung more clues on the sponge and said: "Let's try to do a material that will look the same and will have this quality." And eventually we did it.' Erez continues: 'If you want this material to happen you hire a manufacturer. You have few guys who do material studies, and interesting companies that do this interesting stuff.'[121] The research on materials can be further used for other projects and purposes, not necessarily for this building.

But while designers and manufacturers desperately try to produce a material that would repeat the same effects as generated in the model-making, in order to help the model get closer to the building-to-be, what happens to the building? How does the building travel to get closer to the materials and shapes generated in the studio process? How do these two travellers meet, how do their tentative

115 Interview with Kunlé, November 2002, OMA.
116 Flick House, Zurich, Switzerland, 2001 Museum for contemporary art; commission.
117 Interview with Olga, November 2002, OMA.
118 Interview with Erez, November 2002, OMA.
119 Interview with Ole, November 2002, OMA.
120 Interview with Olga, November 2002, OMA.
121 Interview with Erez, November 2002, OMA.

moves of approaching each other draw trajectories of invention?

Under the pressure of the construction, and in front of the eyes of astonished workers and engineers in Seattle or Porto, architects constantly move back and forth between the building-under-construction and its models, comparing, correcting and simultaneously updating them. 'In Porto, they have a model on the site, because it's such a complicated building that they can go and look at things in the model to better understand it and update it.'[122] 'Even the production phase is still subject to changes,' argues Kunlé. 'So, if we realize that something is totally wrong at that point, we can still change the model *after* the building.'[123] To understand the Seattle Library, for instance, in terms of what the space would look like in three dimensions and to test the diamond seismic system installed between the platforms of the library, as well as the ramps and the fabric of w-sections on the interior of the glass and aluminium skin, the architects built up a mock-up: 'We built the curtain wall, the exterior skin to test it. We did also the book ramp. We basically did one bay of it and we went from ground level, maybe 6 feet high, just to check two different ways of rafting. And even the public was invited to examine it, including disabled people who could test whether they could actually use the wheelchairs.'[124] Models, mock-ups and building stand side by side, and are amended and improved at the same time. This points to the existence of a specific relationship between the models and buildings, as seen under the OMA spotlight. Building and models stand together as two simultaneously present competitive arrangements in architectural design. There is no way to get out of the model without getting into the building, there is no way to get out of the building without getting into the model. The model serves as a way of seeing and envisioning the building because it 'carries a similar spirit or understanding'.[125] Every change in it, every tiny adjustment is meant to influence the building to a certain extent. As architects from OMA put it, the model is made in order to see how it affects the building.

Models and building are associated in such a way that once the architects, clients, and public see the models, they think of the building.

'The building is one moment in the process. And even if you build it, it's just one moment, because of the deadlines. But we always go on and develop it. It's endless. Maybe it also leads to something bad on some occasions. But there is no end to these things. And that's why, when you look at the CCTV and all these models, none of them is really an end product, and none of them is really a beginning, and none of them can stand for the building itself. And everywhere you keep models that look different.'[126]

Thus, the direction of the whole design process is not an ultimate building: instead of beginning with models and ending up with a building in a linear, step-by-step progressive venture, design contains both models and building as two events; each of them is a moment from the becoming of the other, each of them emerges under certain conditions from the other. Both models and building are defined as two states of an active matter, two frozen 'moments' of it: one refines the other as they happily sit at the two ends of the design continuum. Rather than being a *terminus*, the building stands next to its models, coalescent or conterminous with them. That is why a composition of few models is always kept in the office and on the construction site.

If we look more closely at the criss-cross trajectories of models and buildings at the OMA, can we say what the arrow of invention looks like? Does it go from the model to the catalogue, from model effects to novel building materials, from studio events to construction reality? Or, is it perhaps the other way around? Neither the model flies towards

122 Interview with Carol, October 2002, OMA.
123 Interview with Kunlé, November 11, 2002, OMA.
124 Interview with Carol, October 2002, OMA.
125 Interview with Ole, November 2002, OMA.
126 Interview with Erez, November 2002, OMA.

the building in an accelerated course, nor does the building systematically respond to the demands of an experimental model. The model is not an ideal for the building to follow, nor is the building an obedient disciple of the model guidance. Neither imitates or strictly pursues the other. The 'monster model' and the building-to-be run side by side and, in the rush they change pace, they make friends, they respond to other experimental studio events. As a model and a building refer to each other, they trace multifarious trajectories of invention.

Architecture as office enterprise
If we cannot say that the building strives to imitate the model, then we equally cannot maintain the statement that the model is a tool for generating reality. After all, what does it mean to produce realist architecture?[127] No one in the office can answer this question. 'I have always struggled with the term "realistic",' says Ole, 'because I don't know if "realistic" really implies copying any reality, since what one is dealing with is different degrees of abstraction and, as I said, different degrees of interpretation. So, in a certain sense, there is no realistic representation of anything. Architecture remains a process of translation and further definition.'[128]

We can argue for the centrality of the 'the-model-in-the-studio' in the OMA's design. The events in the office generate numerous effects; they introduce life into the studio. Material inventions happen as a re-enactment of studio events. Thus a building is not supposed to represent a reality 'out there'. Instead it tries to repeat, refer to and get closer to life as enacted in the office. It is not description, but enactment that guides the design process at the OMA. The fact that there is no urban life 'out there', far from the studio, has been demonstrated by all those designers who never visited the Whitney site in Manhattan but kept on designing for it, by all those who never learned Spanish but built in Cordoba, and by those who never borrowed a book from the Seattle Library, but reinvented the library typology. Designers never go 'outside'; there is no outside. Manhattan, Seattle, Cordoba are brought into the office; their life is re-enacted in studio practice. The studio constitutes their world. There is no one imaginary Reality within the walls of the office on Heer Bokelweg street,[129] and another Reality outside, but one heterogeneous design world that generates meaning. This story tells us also something about Koolhaas that is often overlooked. It is not by chance that when he looks through the interior glass wall of the office with two doors, the entire world is 'in here'. OMA and Koolhaas treat the studio as the world, a world that is to be re-enacted in practice, a world that is to be reinvented by design.

---

127 Koolhaas's approach is often described as realist: 'Koolhaas knows what his architecture is supposed to look like when materialized. That is, he knows his models and tries, like a realist painter, to make his buildings approach them as closely as possible. He abides by the reality that he has taken as a model, and this is why I have described his architecture as "realist" at some point.' (Moneo, 2004, p. 313).
128 Interview with Ole, November 2002, OMA.
129 That is the Rotterdam address of the Office for Metropolitan Architecture.

In February 2002 Rem took me for an office tour with a small group of museum professionals and curators who had been invited to a presentation. We were all on the ground floor, where the office tour was about to begin. Rem took a small-scale model and rotated it carefully in his hands. Then he stopped for a moment and showed it to Hans-Ulrich who stared at it and, without pausing his camera for a second, said: 'This is the Porto building isn't it?' 'Yes,' replied Rem, and he told the story of the Porto model. The design originated in a commission for a house in suburban Rotterdam several years ago. The client, qualified by Rem as 'a typical Dutch Calvinist', was obsessed by order and tidiness and demanded a neat living area. The house designed by the OMA looked like a hunk of chiselled rock, mounted on a big turntable to follow the sun. But the client was not happy with the design and he dropped the project just as the OMA was entering a design competition for the Porto concert hall. Thus, the abandoned and temporarily forgotten model of the private house came up to the office and re-entered the cycles of design. Lingering on the tables of models for months, it was finally taken with new assumptions, reshaped, refreshed and adjusted. Blowing up its scale and adapting it, the core became the main auditorium, with the foyers, rehearsal halls and offices packed into the leftover space around it. That is how a rejected concept was modified to accommodate a concert hall. It entered a competition and won it: the Casa da Música in Porto.

One would never expect such a mundane story of invention to be told. Stories of reuse, of scaling up of rejected concepts, of recollecting and recycling existing models are not told that often, and certainly not in public. What we usually hear is stories of daring visions, of bold leaps of imagination, of ground-breaking ideas traversing the designers' minds. Why is the Porto story so interesting? What can this kind of story tell us about the office culture? How can this mundane story of reuse inform us of what design invention is about? Going back to the office, we can hear how architects reflect upon and recollect the effects of the Porto example. Ethnographically speaking, I contemplate the importance of this case as related to the office working habits and the particular model-inspired process of design invention.

Having been produced for the private Dutch client, the model travelled only from Rotterdam to its suburban areas to meet the needs of a single person. Being the main mediator in their relationships, the model played an important role in negotiations, sustaining every trace of discussion – be it a trace of disagreement or collective decision. The shift in scale after it was reused and adapted for the concert hall in Porto greatly modified the trajectory of the model. It now had to travel further to meet the needs of creating a more dynamic communal experience, rather than respond only to the demands of a single client. In its scaled up-version, the model served as a mediator between architects and city planning commissions, Porto and Rotterdam, engineers and clients. The model travelled to Portugal on numerous occasions and came back transformed. It always travelled with many other visuals, which were exhibited along with it, and different public groups were invited to assess them. The bigger the number of actors involved in its evaluation, the more complex the models' trajectory became.

Interpreting the trajectory of the Porto model, architects situated it within the overall office project life: 'Porto became the first building of the OMA new line. We have the OMA classic line, and OMA shape-Y line. Like Nike (hahaha). Porto was the first building that was shape-Y. I mean expressive in form. Cordoba followed the line, as did Flick and Whitney, whereas LACMA will be a classic project. This means that the idea is cast in a simple shape. The Embassy in Berlin will be also a classical shape.'[130] Thus, not only the specific material trajectory of the Porto model is taken seriously in the office but it is also inter-preted as playing an important role in the social trajectory of the OMA, and is considered significant in the office life cycle of design inventions.

To unravel the Porto story of reuse, let us go back to the OMA setting. In its dense foam environment, models and try-outs are '… thrown everywhere', explains Erez as we tour the office together, 'so that somebody else can use them for another project or for another experiment.'[131] They can capture time, unfold space, and seize the designers' attention. The models spark their imaginations and make them gather around. As traces of the design process, they are carefully maintained in the office environment so that they could be reappraised and used again for other design projects, for exhibitions or publications. A new shape can emerge as a result of material synergies of exiting co-iso-lated bubbles. An abandoned foam try-out or study model will linger on the tables or the shelves of the office, and 'Rem could pick it a week later with different assumption. And then, there is something that would be difficult to define. It would be, I think, the successful something when aesthetics and intelligence come together with the model.'[132] Yet, if there is *something* in a model that allows architects *to go back* to it and rediscover its potential, the question that increases my curiosity is: how often does this happen in design? Does the Porto story tell us any-thing in particular about the OMA and about the nature of design? Or is it just an exclusive story, fancied by Rem and disliked by most of the designers at the OMA, of how a small Dutch model was scaled up and changed its meaning on the way to Porto?

I quickly noticed that the list of the stories of reuse could be extended further. The Guangzhou Opera House was the result of reuse of an old opera project called Kadi that the office developed but did not win: 'And it was a little bit different, but Rem wanted to go back to the same initial idea. So, we just took it. And I don't know who did the first shape, but it came from there. Somebody sketched it ten years ago, I am sure, or maybe took a piece of foam to build it.[133] Looking at the extended list of reused projects I compiled in my notes, I started examining the models in the office through different eyes. Instead of wondering 'What is the idea behind it?' I asked 'What is the "something" architects go *back to*?' or 'What is it that architects reinterpret and reassemble anew and afresh in these models?'

These stories of reuse show that even if a building is not to be realized, it is still important for OMA architects to keep the traces of design, as new design solutions are imprinted in the models, and the foam try-outs materialize precious design insights. Going back and reusing an old, concept-bearing model is synonymous with efficiency. It reassures the architects that all the efforts and work invested will be rewarded, that the research that has been done and the ideas that emerged will not die, and that the sleepless nights spent in the company of a foam-cutter, a computer and a couple of fellow architects from the same bubble have not been in vain. They can be used for another project; they can have a life.

It is also important for designers to have a good starting point, when struggling to generate a new idea by interacting with a chunk of foam or a computer.

'In design process we also need the previous things to arrive at this stage. You cannot just create an intelligent scheme out of the blue. When you do design, even the schemes that are abandoned, hundreds of models, can be recognized within the process. They are just the different steps in the process.'[134]

Design does not start from scratch. The models at OMA are not only kept because they can be recycled in design – and for that they are deliberately maintained to create a prolific ontological milieu for design invention – but they

130 Interview with Olga, 17 April 2002, OMA.
131 Interview with Erez, April 2002, OMA.
132 Interview with Olga, October 2002, OMA.
133 Interview with Erez, November 2002, OMA.
134 Interview with Kunlé, September 2002, OMA.

also enable different forms of reuse, which never grow up into stories as glorious as the Porto story of reuse.

The reuse of an old project or competition entry, typically an unsuccessful one, can concern only distinct elements of it, not the entire concept. For instance, OMA designers used a façade component of Prada San Francisco[135] for scheme B of the NEwhitney project as a basis for further research. That is how the reuse was discussed in the office.

One morning in September 2002, Rem came and informed the Whitney team that 'Prada San Francisco is not going to happen', and he said: 'You can use this material for the skin of Whitney.' A team discussion followed:

EREZ: It's squeezed; we have to clarify the proportions. To do the connections on the ground level; so we can use the Prada San Francisco scheme! It's dramatic… [to the others] Let's look now at this section. Maybe we don't need to add another floor from Prada San Francisco, because here we have only four floors. I don't know how many we have in the original one of Prada and we need all the stages.

KUNLÉ: Rem also talked about the size of the options. Maybe we have to see that. [he points to the diagram]

EREZ: We should look at Prada, maybe there are some initial ideas we don't know. OK. Let's do that. We have the two boxes. In terms of proportions, we have our project and it's successful. So, we can probably use some of the ideas from Prada. But it's up to us to see how we can incorporate these schemes and proportions.

AY: Is that going to change a lot of things in the work on the NEwhitney?

EREZ: No, it's going to change just a little bit. It's normal to put some ideas we have already explored in the office into another project.'[136]

After Rem's intervention and the group discussion that followed, I interviewed Kunlé and Erez separately, questioning especially the habit of reusing an unsuccessful project and implementing it into the on-going NEwhitney design:

KUNLÉ: Every night and day, we want to test different things, test some existing materials to see how they look on different buildings. The façade of Prada is used, because these materials have already been tried and we start by using it, just to test a direction for investigating further possibilities for our project. I'm sure we are going to use Prada just as a direction for research.[137]

EREZ: You can use the precedents of different things in the office because you have them. It doesn't mean that you use the ideas. When they were done, they had their own ideas; their own things that made an idea evolve. And we have just looked at this now: 'OK, what if it was like that?' We take this as a starting point, as a reference to the building, as an element of the building. But sometimes you take different elements and ideas from other projects. The Porto project was exactly that: it was a small house that had never been built, and we took the entire project. Yes, it's happening, especially in a laboratory like the OMA. You know, you talk to people, you experiment, you go around, you see what is happening in the other projects. It's not that you sit in front of your computer and you don't know what is going on around you.[138]

In the legendary Porto case, which nearly every designer I interviewed mentioned in one way or another, the entire project was reused; scaled up, adapted to different uses, the entire project travelled to Porto. In the Prada-Whitney case, the perspective of reuse makes the project travel only a shorter distance – from one table of models to another, from the Prada to the Whitney working bubble. While travelling across adjacent models within the OMA, reuse means testing a direction to investigate further design possibilities rather than a direct implementation of one

135 Prada San Francisco, San Francisco, USA, 2000; New Prada Headquarters on the West Coast; study.
136 Team discussion, September 2002, OMA
137 Interview with Kunlé, September 2002, OMA.
138 Interview with Erez, September 2002, OMA.

project into another. Thus, when architects talk about reusing an element, they do not mean literally taking an element as such, removing the Prada façade and sticking it to the NEWhitney model, thus repeating it without transformations in a different design context, but rather using it as a basis for further explorations, testing and developing new design directions. Recent projects by OMA, be they successful, dismissed or on hold, work as a conceptual environment for designing architects, and serve as enticement for furthering design research. They have a life in the 'laboratory space' of the OMA before retiring to the quiet archival boxes. The one-room space with no strict boundaries between projects facilitates fruitful encounters among various project bubbles. It enables things to fly across tables and have a happy landing on another table where they trigger a new starting point of design investigation. Here again, the crowded foam environment works as an inspiring milieu for the current projects, stimulating invention.

That is how an office style is generated: to use the Prada idea for the Whitney, designers from the Whitney bubble have to learn what the Prada concept was about. This is the outcome of another working bubble that they will reinsert in an ongoing project. This ensures continuity and efficiency, trains the architects and generates something that will be defined post-factum by the architectural critics as being the OMA style. The practice of reuse also generates an internal infra-language in the office – a particular language especially created by the designers to facilitate understanding and communication when things fly between bubbles. As Olga explains, they often say: 'Shall we do it more like Pinault,[139] or should it be more like the Kunsthal?'[140] Rem also wants to reuse things and to change simultaneously. 'He is greedy with inventions.'[141] The projects are used as point of reference to a certain design specificity – site solution, a material invention or anything else – that can further inspire the design process. According to the architects at the OMA, this specific office infra-language is reminiscent of a playground language.

Alain tells us that the reuse of models could stem initially from a misunderstanding:

ALAIN: Foam models *spark* your imagination much more then computer models usually do. We have also had situations, when one misinterpretation of models turned up in a solution for a building.

AY: That's really very interesting. Can you give an example?

ALAIN: 'I am thinking of Seattle Library. I didn't do it, but my friend did it. They made a model of something and it was *misinterpreted* as the whole building and (...) Do you know the library? It's really a beautiful building. And then it became a solution.[142]

Misinterpretation and mistakes allow new shapes to be created and open up new possibilities for the building-to-be by triggering scenarios unforeseen in the initial architectural plans. They point out the delicately achieved balance between the manipulation of the foam matter and its result, which, combined with differences in the dexterity of execution, make the scale models of the building extremely diverse.

EREZ: I think that models also allow more mistakes. And when we make mistakes, we also find something, and when you find something, it's another opportunity.

AY: Can you give me an example of how you discover something new for the building after making mistakes with models?

EREZ: Sometimes you do something and then by mistake, you say 'ooops', and you put it aside, and somebody sees it and sees another idea in what you did. That's what happened with this model of NATO. And it's always happening in the office. That is also another advantage of the models – that there are always mistakes. If you

139 Fondation Pinault, Paris, France, 2001; private museum on site of the famous Renault factory; competition.

140 Kunsthal, Rotterdam, Netherlands, 1992; museum for temporary exhibitions; built.

141 Interview with Olga, October 2002, OMA.

142 Interview with Alain, 17 April 2002, OMA.

want to experiment, this office allows you to do it. That's why it works. There is a period of time during the design when you can experiment. I think that Rem is aware of that and he lets us do these things.[143]

In the interviews with Sarah, the NATO model is often mentioned as an example of a mistake:

SARAH: One specific example of a mistake that I can remember is that Erez made a model, a kind of conceptual model for a conference room during the NATO project. Even though it wasn't a final option, a complete option, we said 'OK, we are going to develop this and go with this option.' There were a lot of things we liked in it, especially the quality of the light penetrating the model and the way it created space within it, the space below the conference centre. And so, along with the mistake you can make discoveries. We take these things, we discover and translate those into ideas for the next model and the next options.[144]

Thus the NATO model seems to be the perfect example of discovering through mistakes. The bubbles in the model were also produced by mistake, as other architects recall. One of the designers tried to cast transparent material inside the large blocks but it didn't move out. Then one of the girls from the NATO team saw this and came out with the idea of setting the transparent material the other way round. So, following the failure, they inversed the initial concept and placed the concaves inside the model. That particular mistake also helped the architects develop the final competition models made of closed boxes with bowls situated within the box structures. The malleability of foam makes it difficult to cut at a particular angle, thus entailing tentative and accidental gestures, even failures, in the execution of numerous model-making operations. Yet this is also the reason why architects use this particular material to think with – as a quick mediator of both successful and unsuccessful execution. Mistakes also happen in the process of manipulating other materials, in casting and interpreting the first try-outs. They are significant because they redefine the experimental conditions, and allow new configurations of assumptions. As Ole explains: 'You should not lock yourself into the acceptance of certain assumptions and hope for slick interpretations only. We are not afraid of making a lot of mistakes along the way and I think anybody who doesn't do anything wrong also doesn't do anything right. It's an essential part of the process to accept that certain things have to go wrong in order to enable something really right to happen.'[145] To understand this relationship between making models and making mistakes, between doing and undergoing, is to think architecturally.

Thus, architects share one understanding of design invention: You cannot create an intelligent building out of the blue. The new shape stems from an old model, a mistake, a misunderstanding, or a set of existing intricate constraints. Invention happens in meticulous experimentation with the blue foam, carefully archiving, classifying and preserving the models, then reusing, reassessing and weighing them up against other projects and criteria, interpreting and misinterpreting them so that they gradually acquire new meaning. Creating requires architects to recollect and to recycle, to interpret and to repeat, to redefine and reassemble. In the process of doing this, new ideas spark the designers' imagination, new shapes emerge.

To design is to recycle

This short story of model reuse provides a different understanding of design. Rather than being a simple projection of bright ideas and daring leaps of the designer's imagination, or of social and cultural contexts, the new shape emanates as an original and locally perceived form of attachment, connecting and interrelating designers, gestures, objects, bodies and materials in the tentative

143 Interview with Erez, April 2002, OMA.
144 Interview with Sarah, April 2002, OMA.
145 Interview with Ole, June 2002, OMA.

process of design. There is nothing novel and radical in the acts of design invention that were witnessed in the office. To generate a new design concept or building does not imply an *ex nihilo* creation. Instead, the stories of reuse tell us, design means to redesign. Imitation and reiteration constitute the matrix of invention. As Ole summarized this feature of design: 'It is a process of continuous redoing. Nothing is built to represent, but everything is redone. Quantity of foam does not mean a lack of intelligence in a certain sense. I think it is not a process of endless try-outs and errors, but continuous redefinition of what the actual parameters or ambitions of the project are. It is important to be able to learn and see what is fruitful and what has simply come into the end of its own life cycle, and then just continue and requestion, reinterpret the building from this.'[146] Thus, reusing, recollecting, reinterpreting, adapting, remaking – these are all synonyms for creating.

It is impossible to describe the process of invention as being separate from the course of design. As a building praised by the critics for its intellectual ardour and sensual beauty, the Porto Casa da Musica can still be treated as a perfect expression of Koolhaas's vision. Yet, behind the eulogy and the enthusiasm of the critics, there is a mundane story of reuse and recycling, of reinterrogation and reinterpretation, that is to be told in the context of design practice and reconnected to design experience. There is no real disjunction between the designers' ideas and their material practices. To understand a building we need to reconnect visions and design routines, imagination and mistakes.

---

146 Interview with Ole, June 2002, OMA.

Reconnecting Practice And Meaning

In the prevailing analyses of contemporary architectural theory and critique, buildings are interpreted as being separate from both the conditions of their making and the design experience of the makers. A wall of critical interpretations is built around them, rendering their general significance almost opaque. Whenever one talks about the theoretical influences upon Koolhaas's work, whenever one speculates on how the culture he is building for is reflected in a built structure or an urban concept, one quickly realizes that architecture is being remitted to a separate realm, cut off from that vital association with design materials and experiences. This compartmentalization brings about separation of design practice from insight, of imagination from making. Whenever an account of Koolhaas's work tackles his great urban ideas, powerful insights or creative imagination sparked by a variety of psychological or social factors, his design practice is disregarded and the design performance of his office is rarely tackled as being significant for the understanding of his buildings and design concepts.

The stories told here aimed at establishing connections between some OMA projects and the design experiences that accompanied their making; connections of sense, need of enactment and action, of meaning and matter. Traced as two-way associations, they tangled between mundane OMA design trajectories and different societies and cultures, moving constantly from the knower to the known, always afraid of being interrupted, unfaithful or wrong, displaying the knower and the known and the work needed to interrupt or create connections between the OMA and the world. Thus, at any moment in this small ethnography of the OMA, we did not witness a radical shift from face-to-face interactions to macrostructures or abstract contexts *outside* architecture, from pixels on the computer screen or the models in the archive boxes to genuine cultures, societies, nations. We rather kept the same method for all the levels. Follow the architects, their tentative moves, failures and mistakes, their meanderings, cautious search for new materials, adjustments of instruments, scenarios for reuse; *here* is the social element (it is not 'out there'), it is in all those simplified, routinized, repetitive elements.[147] It is not made *outside* the practice of Koolhaas, but *within* the office: in the process of making and scaling a model, recycling a piece of foam, retouching an image on the computer screen; these are all social phenomena. A sense of American culture or Chinese modernity can be gained in the process of making and scaling models, circulating, classifying and archiving them, sustaining and reusing foam, recollecting visuals on the tables of models, in design reports and concept books. To understand the societies produced by architects, we need to look at them from the inside out.

The stories I told here also made an attempt to restore continuity between the intensified form of experience that a design work is and the everyday events, doings, trails, sufferings, mistakes that are part of design experience. To understand architecture, one must begin with it in the raw. If we talk about a project, its accomplishment, its end, would be the simple coincidence of the initial models and their final realization. Yet, unravelling how a building happens and travels in design is the opposite of showing how precisely it has been created and realized. *Trajectory* stands for the opposite of what a *project* is. Following the trajectories of 'monster models' and buildings, architects and foam, we witnessed no gradual progression toward reality, no realization of plans and projects, but vertiginous hesitation, fundamental meandering of architects and visuals, going back and reworking, recollecting and recycling, rather than going forward and projecting in time. The different trajectories traced here show the richness of design reality and the different modes of existence of design works.

By choosing the genre of short stories, my intentions were humble: I did not try to explain the OMA practice or Koolhaas's approach; nor did I attempt to grapple with the genuine nature of design. This genre was used here with the pure purpose of generating infra-reflexive descriptions of invention which would keep the freshness of design experiences and even the roughness of the design language far from the reach of the prevailing meta-reflexive theories of design. Deliberately circumventing any meta-reflexivity that would have increased the layers of methodological reflections, I simply described various design practices without sticking to references outside architecture, while also relying on the assumption that these infra-reflexive accounts will be self-exemplifying.

Drawing on mundane stories of design, I showed how innovation permeates design practice, how everyday techniques become central to design across projects and set standards for the way in which buildings and urban phenomena are to be seen, the way a building emerges and becomes graspable, real. It is an attempt to track architectural invention, which is usually considered to be abstract, via the concrete details of the architectural practice. It does not exist only as an ideal for architectural excellence, but as a number of workaday choices: which instrument to use, whether or not to retouch a photograph with Photoshop, which model to reuse, how to stage a presentation, which archives to pick up, which option to eliminate. In the mundane stories of invention recalling these choices, the Hurrah-moments of architecture-making were missing; they were replaced by routine gestures of model-making, recycling, assembling, recollecting, discussing, rescaling.

Having followed these stories, can you still explain design in terms of creation and construction? No. Not any longer. 'Creator' always implies an architect standing at the beginning of the creation vector, originating a creation. 'Creation' implies a genius able to create *ex nihilo*. Designing requires many more skills as well as obsessive attention to the details instead of relying on the flight of subjective imagination and the grand gestures of emanci-

---

147 Here I follow Bruno Latour's understanding of the social as a connecting element rather than as a separate domain (See Latour, 2005b).

pated creativity. A building is not obtained in a double-click instant of creation or construction, but through numerous little operations of shaping the foam, scaling it and refining its texture, adjusting the foam-cutters and other devices, classifying and reusing old models, struggling to repeat tentative experimental results and generate a new material. Therefore to grasp architectural work required for our stories, it was essential to devote meticulous attention to the specific trajectories of models, to the minute movements of the foam, to the various ways a model compels its makers, to the series of dismissed projects, to the unfortunate moves of execution.

The problem of interpretation of Koolhaas's architecture is, I argue, rooted in his practice – he is not the discoverer, the unique creator, but one of the inventors of these buildings-to-be. Let the critics still interpret his architecture through the narrow meta-reflexive lens of the irreducible uniqueness of his personality, Surrealism-inspired, rooted in his Dutch-ness and individual approach. The master architect is not a lone genius,[148] but the setter of a specific studio practice; his buildings are born in the studio world. There is no solitary perception or self-examination; design takes place within a larger spectrum, mobilizing the senses of many, just as the construction of a building is always distributed within a collective of engineers, builders, contractors, building committees, users and architects. Follow the trajectories of models and architects and you can witness the centrality of the studio in the process of invention at the OMA. The entire OMA design work revolves around life as it is staged in the office: in model-making, in the travels of the model, in studio events and situations of reuse. There, the architects are performers and spectators and architecture becomes part of the performance that we view.

The stories told here also demonstrate the irrelevance of the modernist opposition between what is social, symbolic, subjective, lived, and what is material, real, objective and factual. In architectural theory, design easily lends itself to semiotics: it is made to be interpreted in terms of language of signs. Yet, a close look at design practices shows that there are no two distinctive ways of grasping an architectural object, i.e., one through its intrinsic materiality, the other through its more aesthetic or 'symbolic' aspects. To design is not simply to add meaning to a brute, passive, and technical matter. The materiality of every OMA project, of every model or foam try-out, spreads a meaning with it.

The stories also outlined that design never starts from scratch. There is no need for the creative process to be entirely revolutionized, for the architect to have absolute mastery over the materials, to predict experiments without mistakes. Design experience suggests an undertone of modesty that is never accounted for with care and respect – it does not require grand gestures of radical departure from the past, but small operations of re-collecting existing bits of projects and concepts, reusing, recycling, reinterpreting, rethinking; the 're-' stands at the heart of design. There is no fundamental break with architectural conventions or accumulated office traditions. No audacious rule-violation is needed for a new design to emerge. Rather, there are small repetitive routines; there is always something modest and something counteractive in design.

Opposing arbitrary symbolic meaning and 'mere matter' will not lead us to a better understanding of architecture. If critical thinkers still argue that the Porto building is a unique expression of Koolhaas's most audacious thinking, a building whose intellectual ardour is matched by its sensual beauty, or qualify the Seattle Library as a deconstructivist building *par excellence*, the bravest civic project in the USA over the last couple of decades, all these interpretations do is to segregate the symbolic features of these buildings from their material and physical aspects, from the tentative trajectories of their models and the ontolog-

---

148 On architectural creativity as emerging in a moment of solitude, delirium and concealment, see Silvetti, 1982.

ical vibrancy of the OMA architectural environment. No euphoric eulogy or overjoyed interpretations of finished design works, of buildings that are constructed and urban concepts that are being tested, can assist their understanding. If you happen to be in Seattle you can still enjoy the Public Library there without knowing anything about the design experiments that took place in the OMA some years before it was built, without witnessing the trajectory of its model, the test of the micro-diamond pattern of the metal mesh and the mock-up of the ramp. If you happen to be in Porto, you can still enjoy the Casa da Musica without knowing anything about the tribulations of its scale model and its metamorphoses from a Dutch private house to a public building in Portugal. You can still appreciate a building, like or dislike it, praise or dismiss it, without knowing anything about the design experience that made it happen; but you cannot *understand* a building without taking these design experiences into account.

References

Alpers, Svetlana, *Rembrandt's Enterprise. The Studio and the Market*, London 1988, Thames & Hudson Ltd.

Becker, Howard S., 'Art As Collective Action', *American Sociological Review* 1974, 39(6): 767-76.

Becker, Howard. S., *Art Worlds*, Berkeley 1982, University of California Press.

Blau, Judith R., *Architects and Firms: a Sociological Perspective on Architectural Practice*, Cambridge 1984, MIT Press.

Bonfilio, Paul, *Fallingwater: the Model*, New York 2000, Rizzoli.

Borden, I. and Rendell, J. (eds.), *Inter Sections: Architectural Histories and Critical Theories*, London and New York 2000, Routledge.

Bourdieu, Pierre, 'The Berber House', pp. 98-110, in M. Douglas (ed.), *Rules and Meanings: An Anthropology of Everyday Knowledge*, Harmondsworth 1971, Penguin.

Bredekamp, in Rappolt, M. and Violette, R. (eds.), *Gehry Draws*, MIT Press, 2005.

Busch, Akiko, *The Art of the Architectural Model*, New York 1991, Design Press.

Callon, Michel, 'Le travail de la conception en architecture', *Situations Les Cahiers de la recherche architecturale* (37) 1996, 25-35.

Chaslin, Francois, *Deux conversation avec Rem Koolhaas et caetera*, Paris 2001, Sens & Tonka.

Colquhoun, Alan, *Essays in Architectural Criticism: Modern Architecture and Historical Change*, Cambridge 1981, MIT Press.

Crickhowell, Nicholas, *Opera House lottery. Zaha Hadid and the Cardiff Bay Project*, Cardiff 1997, University of Wales Press.

Cuff, Dana, *Architecture: the Story of Practice*, Cambridge 1991, MIT Press.

Cuito, Aurora and Cristina Montes (eds.), *Rem Koolhaas: OMA (Archipockets)*, Kempen 2002, Neues Publishing Company.

Damisch, Hubert, 'The Manhattan Transfer', in Lucan, Jacques,

OMA – *Rem Koolhaas. Architecture 1970-1990*, New York 1991,
Princeton Architectural Press, pp. 21-33.
Deleuze, Gilles and Felix Guattari, *A Thousand Plateaus*,
Minneapolis 1987, University of Minnesota Press.

Evans, Robin, *The Fabrication of Virtue: English Prison Architecture*,
1750-1840, Cambridge Cambridgeshire, New York 1982,
Cambridge University Press.
Evans, Robin, *Translations from Drawing to Building*,
Cambridge 1997, MIT Press.
Evans, Robin, 'Architectural Projection' in Eva Blau and Edward
Kaufman (eds.), *Architecture and Its Image*, Montreal 1989, 19-35.

Fisher, Thomas, *In the Scheme of Things: Alternative Thinking on
the Practice of Architecture*, Minneapolis 2000, University of
Minnesota Press.
Foucault, Michel, *Discipline and Punish: the Birth of the Prison*.
London 1979, Penguin Books.

Galison, Peter and Emily Thompson (eds.), *The Architecture of
Science*, Mass., London 1999, MIT Press.
Guattari, Felix, 'Les machines architecturales de Shin Takamatsu,'
in *Chimères* 21, 1994, pp. 127–41.

Hays, K. Michael, *Architecture Theory Since 1968*, Cambridge 1998,
MIT Press.
Heath, Tom, *Method in Architecture*, Chichester 1984, Wiley.
Heurtin, Jean-Philippe, *L'espace publique parlamentaire. Essai sur les
raisons du législateur.* Paris 1999, Presses Universitaires de France.
Hill, Jonathan, *Actions of Architecture: Architects and Creative Users*,
London 2003, Routledge.
Houdart, Sophie, 'Des multiples manières d'être reel – Les
représentations en perspective dans le projet d'architecture',
in *Terrain* 46, 2006, pp. 107-22.
Houdart, Sophie and Chihiro Minato, *Kuma Kengo. Essai de
monographie décalée*, Paris 2009, Editions donner lieu.
Hubbard, Bill, *A Theory for Practice: Architecture in Three Discourses*,
Cambridge 1995, MIT Press.

James, William, Pragmatism: A New Name for Some Old Ways   **109**
of Thinking, New York 1907, Longman Green and Co.

Jencks, Charles and George Baird (eds.), *Meaning in Architecture*,
London 1969, Barrie & Rockliff the Cresset P.

Johnson, Paul-Alan, *The Theory of Architecture: Concepts,
Themes & Practices*, New York 1994, Van Nostrand Reinhold.

Jones, J. Christopher, *Design Methods: Seeds of Human Futures*,
London 1970, Wiley-Interscience.

King, Anthony D., *Buildings and Society: Essays on the Social
Development of the Built Environment*, London 1980,
Routledge & Kegan Paul.

King, Anthony D., *The Bungalow: the Production of a Global Culture*,
London 1984, Routledge & Kegan Paul.

Koolhaas, Rem, *Delirious New York: a Retroactive Manifesto for
Manhattan*, London 1978, Thames and Hudson.

Koolhaas, Rem, and others, *Small, Medium, Large, Extra-large*,
Rotterdam 1995, 010 Publishers.

Kwinter, Sanford (ed.), *Rem Koolhaas. Conversations with students*,
Rice University School of Architecture, Houston,
Texas & New York 1996, Princeton Architectural Press.

Latour, Bruno, 'The Politics of Explanation: An alternative',
in Woolgar, S. (ed.), *Knowledge and Reflexivity: New Frontiers
in the Sociology of Knowledge* 1988, 155-77.

Latour, Bruno, *Pandora's Hope: an Essay on the Reality of Science
Studies*, Cambridge 1999, Harvard University Press.

Latour, Bruno (2005a), 'En tapotant légèrement sur l'architecture
de Koolhaas avec un bâton d'aveugle', Architecture
d'aujourd'hui, Nov-Dec, no.361, pp.70-9.

Latour, Bruno (2005b), *Reassembling the Social: an Introduction to
Actor-Network-Theory*, Oxford, Oxford University Press.

Latour, Bruno and Albena Yaneva, 'Give me a gun and I will make
all buildings move: an ANT's view of architecture', in Geiser
R. (ed), *Explorations in Architecture: Teaching, Design, Research*,
Basel 2008, Birkhäuser.

Lawson, Bryan, *Design in Mind*, Oxford 1994, Butterworth
Architecture.

110 Leach, Neil (ed.), *Rethinking Architecture*, London and New York
1997, Routledge.

Levene, Richard, Fernando Marquez Cecilia, Rem Koolhaas,
OMA*AMO, *Rem Koolhaas 1996-2006, I: delirious and more = delirio
y mas*, Madrid 2006, El Croquis.

Lucan, Jacques, OMA – *Rem Koolhaas. Architecture 1970-1990*,
New York 1991

Markus, Thomas, *Buildings and Power*. London and New York
1993, Routledge.

Mical, Thomas, *Surrealism and Architecture*, London 2005,
Routledge.

Mitchell, C. Thomas, *New Thinking in Design: Conversations on
Theory and Practice*, New York 1996, Van Nostrand Reinhold.

Moneo, Rafael, *Theoretical Anxiety and Design Strategies in the Work
of Eight Contemporary Architects*, Cambridge, Mass. 2004,
MIT Press, 306-59.

Muthesius, S., *The English Terraced House*, New Haven and London
1982, Yale University Press.

Ockman, Joan (ed.), *Architecture, Criticism, Ideology*, Princeton N.J.
1985, Princeton Architectural Press.

Office for Metropolitan Architecture and Rem Koolhaas, *Content*,
Cologne 2004, Taschen.

Patteeuw, Veronique (ed.), *What is OMA? Considering Rem Koolhaas
and the Office for Metropolitan Architecture*, Rotterdam 2004,
NAi publishers.

Pollack, Sydney, *Esquisses de Frank Gehry*, SP Architecture
Productions LLC 2006, Princeton Architectural Press.

Porter, Tom, *How Architects Visualize*, New York 1979,
Van Nostrand Reinhold.

Porter, Tom & John Neale, *Architectural Supermodels: Physical
Design Simulation*, Oxford 2000, Architectural Press.

Robbins, Edward, *Why Architects Draw*, Cambridge, London 1994,
MIT Press.

Rowe, Peter G., *Design Thinking*, Cambridge 1987, MIT Press.

Schön, Donald A., *The Reflective Practitioner: How Professionals*   **111**
Think in Action, New York 1983, Basic Books.

Schön, Donald A., *The Design Studio: an Exploration of its Traditions
and Potentials*, London 1985, RIBA Publications.

Shoshkes, Ellen, *The Design Process*, New York 1989, Whitney
Library of Design.

Silvetti, Jorge, 'Representation and Creativity in Architecture:
The Pregnant Moment', in O. Akin and E. G. Weinel (eds.),
Representation and Architecture, 1982, Silver Spring, pp. 159-84.

Sloterdijk, Peter, *Ecumes: Spheres III, Spherologie plurielle*, Paris 2005,
Maren Sell Editeurs.

Souriau, Etienne, 'Du mode d'existence de l'œuvre à faire', *Bulletin
de la société française de philosophie*, 25 February 1956, pp. 4-44.

Tafuri, Manfredo, *Architecture and Utopia: Design and Capitalist
Development*, Mass., London 1979, MIT Press.

Tarde, Gabriel, *Monadologie et sociologie*, Paris 1999 (reprint),
Les Empecheurs de parler end rond.

Venturi, Robert and Denise Scott Brown, *Architecture as Signs and
Systems*, Cambridge 2004, Belknap Press of Harvard University
Press.

Vidler, Anthony, *The Architectural Uncanny: Essays in the Modern
Unhomely*, Cambridge, Mass. 1992, MIT Press.

Yaneva, Albena, 'Scaling up and Down: Extraction Trials in Architectural Design', in *Social Studies of Science* (35) 2005, 867-94.

Yaneva, Albena, *The Making of a Building: A Pragmatist Approach
to Architecture*, Oxford 2009, Peter Lang.

This publication has been made possible by the generous support
of the Netherlands Architecture Fund, the Graham Foundation
for Advanced Studies in the Fine Arts.

ILLUSTRATIONS Albena Yaneva, Manchester
DESIGN Piet Gerards Ontwerpers, Amsterdam
(Piet Gerards and Monique Hegeman)
PRINTING Lecturis, Eindhoven

ISBN 978 90 6450 714 4
www.010.nl

5TH FLOOR GALLERY

WHITNEY (NEW)
1" = 32" ZONING
MODEL
W/ PLEXI
ZONING PROFILE
JULY 2002

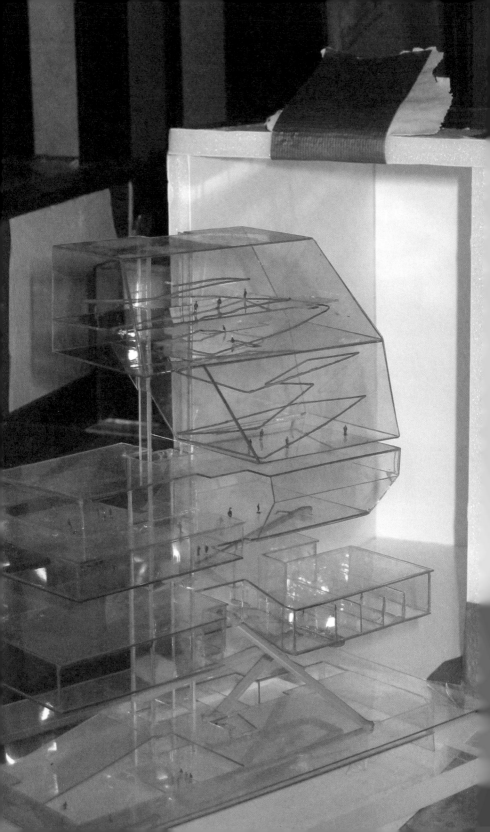